Synchronization of Parallel Programs

MIT Press Series in Scientific Computation
Dennis Gannon, editor

Synchronization of
Parallel Programs

F. André, D. Herman,
and J.-P. Verjus

Translated by
J. Howlett

The MIT Press
Cambridge, Massachusetts

First MIT Press edition, 1985.

English translation © 1985 by NORTH OXFORD ACADEMIC Publishing Company Limited.

Original edition published under the title *Synchronisation de programmes parallèles* by Dunod, France. © BORDAS 1983.

Published in Great Britain by

NORTH OXFORD ACADEMIC Publishing Company Limited
242 Banbury Road
Oxford OX2 7DR
England

Printed in Great Britain

Library of Congress Cataloging in Publication Data
André, Françoise.
    Synchronization of parallel programs.

    (MIT Press series in scientific computation)
    Translation of: Synchronisation de programmes parallèles.
    Bibliography: p.
    Includes index.
    1. Parallel processing (Electronic computers)
I. Herman, Daniel.   II. Verjus, J.-P.   III. Title.
IV. Series.
QA76.6.A4913   1985   001.64   84-26180
ISBN 0-262-01085-2

Contents

v

Series Foreword

It is often the case that periods of rapid evolution in the physical sciences occur when there is a timely confluence of technological advances and improved experimental technique. Many physicists, computer scientists and mathematicians have said that such a period of rapid change is now underway. We are currently undergoing a radical transformation in the way we view the boundaries of experimental science. It has become increasingly clear that the use of large-scale computation and mathematical modelling is now one of the most important tools in the scientific and engineering laboratory. We have passed the point of viewing the computer as a device for tabulating and correlating experimental data; we now regard it as a primary vehicle for testing theories for which no practical experimental apparatus can be built. NASA scientists speak of "numerical" wind tunnels, and physicists experiment with the large-scale structure of the universe.

The major technolgical change accompanying this new view of experimental science is a blossoming of new apprioaches to computer architecture and algorithm design. By exploiting the natural parallelism in scientific applications, new computer designs show the promise of major advances in processing power. When coupled with the current biennial doubling of memory capacity, supercomputers are on the way to becoming the laboratories of much of modern science.

In this series we hope to focus on the effect that these changes are having on the design of mathematical and scientific software. In particular, we plan to highlight many major new trends in the design of numerical algorithms and the associated programming and software tools that are being driven by the new advances in computer architecture. Of course, the relation between algorithm design and computer design architecture is symbiotic. New views on the structure of physical processes demand new computational models, which then drive the design of new machines. We can expect progress in this area for many years, as our understanding of the emerging science of concurrent computation deepens.

One of the least understood problems facing the designers of software for parallel or distributed computer systems is the coordination and synchronization of parallel processes. In this volume André, Herman, and Verjus give a rigorous treatment of both the formal expression of synchronization language constructs and several important implementation issues. In particular, the authors treat the problems of the context of a shared memory multiprocessor as well as physically distributed systems. This book will be of interest to a wide variety of people involved in programming parallel computers.

Dennis B. Gannon

Control of parallelism and distribution

Two factors today exert a major influence on the design and programming of applications: the use of modular and parallel programming languages, and the development of distributed architectures. These two elements lead to the expression of an application as a set of relatively independent processes, rather than as a program executed sequentially.

Depending on the application in question, processes may either describe real physical systems (simulation), or represent real or virtual machines (e.g. the execution of an arithmetical function). Finally, they may control and direct real processes (e.g. control of machine tools). Processes which concurrently implement an application are necessarily linked by *cooperative* relations. Moreover, the implementation of several processes using limited resources (e.g. memory, peripherals, CPUs), leads to problems of *competition*.

In this book, we shall propose a method for expressing typical cooperation and competition problems, as well as different *synchronization and communication* methods for implementing them.

Chapter 1 acts as an introduction to the book, using a simple illustration which stresses the idea we intend to demonstrate, i.e. that we need to express synchronization constraints between parallel processes by means of a statement which we call an abstract expression. Once stated, this abstract expression must be implemented by a 'controller' which may be represented in various ways, e.g. by a monitor representing all the procedures making up the protocol which the processes must respect, or by a process whose role is to enforce that protocol, or again by several cooperating processes. Consequently, we distinguish between two types of implementation: a centralized implementation in which a single entity is responsible for all control operations, as opposed to a distributed implementation in which several entities cooperate to implement control operations. Although it is entirely conceivable that a distributed approach could be implemented within a centralized computing system (one of several processors sharing a common memory), it is more common under these conditions to use a centralized approach. On the other hand, in a distributed system (in general terms, one made up of processors interconnected by a communication medium which is not a common memory), either solution could be adopted.

The book therefore unfolds in a completely natural way, with the three subsequent chapters dealing respectively with languages for the expression of synchronization problems (chapter 2), tools and methods for centralized implementation (chapter 3), and tools and methods for distributed implementation (chapter 4).

Chapters 3 and 4 have the same general structure: methods and principles, fundamental synchronization tools, synchronization techniques. Both end with examples in which the reader will encounter classic problems solved using the methods advocated here: abstract expression — implementation. The problems dealt with are: reader/writer in the centralized implementation, distributed allocation of resources, coherent management of multiple copies of a file in a distributed implementation, avoidance of deadlock in a distributed resource allocation problem, and management of access to a partitioned file in a distributed implementation.

The reader will also find a number of classic problems dealt with in the course of the text, such as mutual exclusion for access to a resource, or the producer/consumer problem. Finally, the example described informally in the introduction (that of management of access to a swimming pool) reappears throughout the book and acts as something of a 'leitmotif'.

Chapter 1

Introduction

1.1. The problem

For a particular application, the cooperating processes will be aware of each other's existence and their cooperative interactions will be defined explicitly. In contrast, any competitive interactions between processes will be indirect because, in this respect, the processes are unaware of each other. This distinction holds only at a given level of observation; if the implementation is realized in successive levels, the relations between the processes can be different at each level. The resolution of a competitive situation may, for example, require the creation of cooperating processes; conversely, cooperating processes could compete with one another for resources.

Example 1

Consider a set of processes $\{P\}$ which share a single printer. Access to this printer is gained by cooperation between the calling processes of $\{P\}$, on the one hand, and a single print-server process, on the other.

Example 2

Suppose there is a set of processes which cooperate in pairs to produce and print certain values. The cooperative interactions between the producer and printer processes of each pair are expressed in terms of the procedures GET and PUT, which handle access to the values stored in a buffer.

Since the buffers for all the producer–printer pairs must reside in a store with limited capacity, the process pairs will compete for storage locations indirectly by means of GET and PUT.

This competition can be resolved by cooperation between the processes which allocate and retrieve the buffer space.

For whatever reason, the processes interact with one another and communicate, possibly only by means of simple signals. We are concerned with the synchronization of the processes involved in this information exchange. We shall use the term **controller** for an abstract entity to which all the processes to be synchronized are linked, and the term **system** for processes and controller viewed as a whole.

1

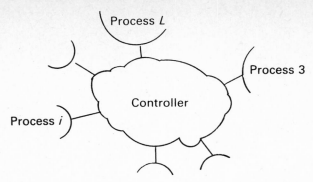

Fig. 1. *A system.*

We consider the processes as taking place in discrete steps, or, if they are continuous, as being sampled for observation at discrete intervals. At each step there is an **event**, which can be either local to the process in which it occurs and not perceived by the rest of the system, or can have some significance for the whole system, in which case it is relevant to the general problem of synchronization. We shall consider only events of this second type, and we lay down the following definition:

> *Synchronization consists of controlling the evolution of processes, and therefore the occurrence of events, as a function of the past history of the system.*

We shall consider systems for which the time interval between any pair of events can be ignored, each process being represented by a series of events. We define **logical synchronization** (as distinct from synchronization in real time) to be the establishment of some form of agreement between a number of processes, each of which has arrived at a given event. This agreement is imposed only at that point, and the processes then continue at their own rates until the next synchronization point is reached.

Note: There are problems in real time in which the interval between events is significant. For example, in telephony, when the caller (here, the control process) gets the dialling tone, he must dial the necessary numbers within a limited time; if he takes too long he has to start the process again from the beginning. One way to bring this type of problem within the scope of the above assumption is to represent an interval as a succession of 'pips' from a clock, and to introduce a special process to count such pips; this process allows an event to occur at the required instant. It is this event that has to be considered, not the interval. However, there can still be a practical problem here, in that the event must be dealt with quickly enough by the controller.

Among those systems to which the concept of logical synchronization can be applied, we shall be particularly interested in those for which it is not necessary to retain the complete past history; for these, only a summary of certain significant characteristics need be kept.

Example

Suppose that at every 25th event of class C, a process P must halt and await the occurrence of an event E in a process Q. The significant information here is the number of events of class C which have occurred.

Note 1: The state of a sequential process, observed at some point in its lifetime, will be a function of its past history; generally, this history is summarized in, for example, the values of its variables.

Note 2: It is important not to confuse the problem of synchronization of processes with that of ensuring that each of the processes to be synchronized behaves in a coherent or orderly manner. For example, when there is a single critical resource, the problem of coherence is that of ensuring that no process uses this resource without first having requested it, whilst synchronization is the problem of coordinating the requests made for this resource by the various processes. In the following, we shall consider only coherent processes.

1.2. An introductory example

As a means of introducing the problems of synchronization and the methods and tools available for tackling these problems, especially those provided by information science, we shall develop an example from outside the field; we have taken it from [Latteux 80].

A swimming pool can accommodate a limited number of users, expressed by the number B of baskets available for the swimmers' clothes. Furthermore, both before and after swimming, the users compete for the use of changing cabins of which there are a total of C, with $1 < C \ll B$. Each swimmer is a process and the cabins and baskets are the objects for which they compete.

1.2.1. Representation of a process

A process represents the life history of a swimmer in the system we are considering; this can be expressed as:

begin
    CHANGING
    SWIMMING
    DRESSING
end

This expression says nothing about the resources used, but at this level of description of the system there may be nothing to gain from being more precise. In fact, without a fuller analysis, it is difficult to choose between the following two expressions:

(a)	(b)
GET A BASKET	*GET A BASKET AND A CABIN*
GET A CABIN	*PUT CLOTHES IN BASKET*
PUT CLOTHES IN BASKET	*LEAVE CABIN*
LEAVE CABIN	

There is clearly no need to consider the expression in which the order of the first two operations in (a) is reversed.

In information science terminology we can say that CHANGING and DRESSING are procedures and that they share, i.e. compete for, access to common resources.

The following events can be observed in each process in the total system which includes all the swimmers:

permit	*CHANGING*
end	*CHANGING*
permit	*DRESSING*
end	*DRESSING*

and these are the only events which are significant for the problem, for it is after one or other of these that the state of the resources is modified. We shall see in chapter 2 that it is common for the events

request	*(ACTION)*	(see section 1.2.6)
permit	*(ACTION)*	
end	*(ACTION)*	

to be involved in each action of a process. Here, the action *CHANGING*, which comes between the events *permit CHANGING* and *end CHANGING*, assumes the availability of a basket and a cabin; and similarly for *DRESSING*, which comes between *permit DRESSING* and *end DRESSING*.

If we had gone further into the expression for process (a) above, for example, we should have been led to take note of other events. As we saw in section 1.1, the relations between processes differ according to the level at which they are observed and there are differences, therefore, between the events and the synchronization constraints.

1.2.2. Expressing synchronization

In order to express the constraints imposed by synchronization, we have to find a way to represent the state of the system in terms of observable quantities.

At any instant, the number of cabins occupied is equal to the sum of the number of people changing and the number dressing, i.e.

number_of CABINS OCCUPIED = number_of CHANGING
+ number_of DRESSING

The number of people changing can be expressed in terms of the number of events *permit CHANGING* and *end CHANGING*:

$$number\_of\ CHANGING = number\_of\ permit\ CHANGING$$
$$- number\_of\ end\ CHANGING$$

and in general, for any action X, the number in progress at any instant is:

$$number\_of\ actions\ X\ in\ progress = number\_of\ permit\ X - number\_of\ end\ X$$

The number of baskets occupied is equal to the total number of people in the pool (either in the changing cabins or swimming):

$$number\_of\ BASKETS\ OCCUPIED = number\_of\ permit\ CHANGING$$
$$- number\_of\ end\ DRESSING$$

and the state of the system must satisfy the following constraints, which form the **invariant** of the system:

$$number\_of\ CABINS\ OCCUPIED \leqslant C$$
$$and\ number\_of\ BASKETS\ OCCUPIED \leqslant B$$

The first of these inequalities can be written:

$$number\_of\ permit\ CHANGING - number\_of\ end\ CHANGING$$
$$+ number\_of\ permit\ DRESSING - number\_of\ end\ DRESSING \leqslant C$$

This invariant can be broken by each new *permit* event, and therefore these are the events which the observer (i.e. the controller or synchronizer) must control, whereas he can simply record the others. We therefore write:

condition for permit (CHANGING):

$$number\_of\ CHANGING + number\_of\ DRESSING < C$$
$$and\ number\_of\ permit\ CHANGING - number\_of\ end\ DRESSING < B$$

condition for permit (DRESSING):

$$number\_of\ CHANGING + number\_of\ DRESSING < C$$

This makes the role of the controller clear: he simply records and counts certain events but must intervene in others and delay their occurrence until a particular event allows them to take place.

For the moment, we shall not go further than this conditional expression, or the equivalent invariant. It is not something for which a formal proof has to be given: it is in fact an expression of the problem; however, we shall see in section 1.2.7 that we can give proofs of certain features of the behaviour of a system subjected to these constraints.

1.2.3. Centralized implementation

Implementation is a matter of constructing an **operating mechanism** and attempting to prove that it conforms to the specification of the system. In a centralized implementation, in data processing or in any other context, the

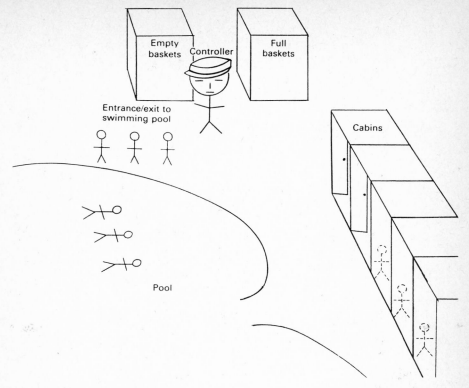

Fig. 2. *Centralized system. The controller is aware of all significant events.*

controller must be a single, privileged observer who is aware of every event. We can envisage a human controller who regulates the handing out of baskets and the allocation of changing cabins; all the swimmers report to him, both on entering and leaving either the building or the pool. His complete knowledge of the system enables him to implement, if he wishes, a more finely structured control policy which could favour either new arrivals or swimmers leaving the pool (see section 1.2.6).

For implementation of the system in computational terms, we can use

either   four counters providing a count to the events listed in section 1.2.1:

permit CHANGING, end CHANGING, permit DRESSING, end DRESSING

or   two counters: *number_of CABINS OCCUPIED, number_of BASKETS OCCUPIED*

The controller can either be explicit, taking the form of a special process (see, for example, Ada [Ichbiah 79; ASRM 83] or a monitor [Hoare 74]), or it can be implicit. In the latter case, the counters are shared variables which each process checks and updates independently of all the others, using semaphores, conditional critical regions, or some other means; we give examples in chapter 3.

To show how easily an implementation can be based on the expression presented in section 1.2.2, we shall state it in Ada [ASRM 83], with no further explanation.

```
task type SWIMMER ;
task body SWIMMER is
   begin
      POOL.CHANGING ;
      ... SWIMMING ... ;
      POOL.DRESSING ;
   end SWIMMER ;
package POOL is
   procedure CHANGING ;
   procedure DRESSING ;        -- several CHANGING and DRESSING
                               -- procedures can be called simultaneously
end POOL ;
```

The pool controller will use two variables whose values are modified at each observed event according to the following table:

	CHANGING		DRESSING	
	permit	end	permit	end
NBRCABINS_OCC	+1	−1	+1	−1
NBRBASKETS_OCC	+1			−1

The procedures CHANGING and DRESSING, and their controller, are as follows:

```
package body POOL is
   task CONTROLLER is
      entry PERM_CHANGING ;       -- these entries are made in
      entry END_CHANGING ;        -- a mutually exclusive manner
      entry PERM_DRESSING ;
      entry END_DRESSING ;
   end CONTROLLER ;

task body CONTROLLER is
   NBRCABINS_OCC, NBRBASKETS_OCC : integer := 0 ;
   begin              -- the body of CONTROLLER is a loop which, at each
                      -- iteration services a call to an entry point;
                      -- acceptance by the entry point is subject to the
                      -- conditions at the time.
```

```
loop
  select
    accept END_CHANGING ; NBRCABINS_OCC
                              := NBRCABINS_OCC − 1 ;
  or
    accept END_DRESSING ; NBRCABINS_OCC
                              := NBRCABINS_OCC − 1 ;
                          NBRBASKETS_OCC
                              := NBRBASKETS_OCC − 1 ;
  or when  NBRCABINS_OCC < C and NBRBASKETS_OCC < B
    accept PERM_CHANGING ; NBRCABINS_OCC
                              := NBRCABINS_OCC + 1 ;
                          NBRBASKETS_OCC
                              := NBRBASKETS_OCC + 1 ;
  or when NBRCABINS_OCC < C
    accept PERM_DRESSING ; NBRCABINS_OCC
                              := NBRCABINS_OCC + 1 ;
  end select
end loop
end CONTROLLER ;

procedure CHANGING is begin PERM_CHANGING ;
                        ... CHANGING ... ;
                        END_CHANGING ;
                      end CHANGING ;
procedure DRESSING is begin  PERM_DRESSING ;
                        ... DRESSING ... ;
                        END_DRESSING ;
                      end DRESSING ;
end POOL ;
```

1.2.4. Difficulties in observing events

The initiation of the action *CHANGING* is conditional on gaining permission to get a basket and a cabin. In the proposed implementation in section 1.2.3, it is assumed that the controller gives both the permission to get a basket, and the basket itself, at the same time. The swimmer, however, may delay using the cabin even though it is allocated to him from the moment he is given the controller's permission. The event 'occupation of a cabin' is not therefore observable by the controller, who substitutes for this the event *permit CHANGING*, which implies that a cabin is liable to be occupied.

Similarly, when a user has finished with his cabin, he may chat with others or wait in the changing area, and thus delay reporting to the controller; the controller does not, therefore, observe the event 'cabin becomes free', but a later event. This is illustrated in Fig. 3.

Thus, according to the abstract specification, control of the system must be

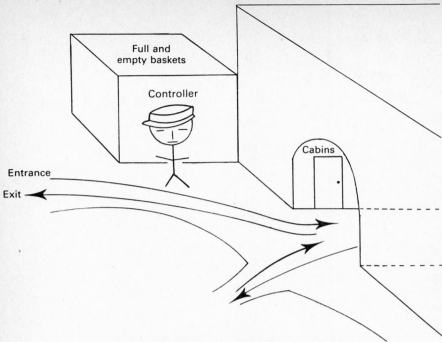

Fig. 3. *Difficulties in observing events.*

achieved by monitoring each entry to, or exit from, a cabin and allocating or retrieving a basket at the entrance and exit of each cabin. As this is difficult to achieve, we choose instead to count and control other events. As far as the organization of cabins is concerned, for example, the events for each process are considered in time order, as follows:

Observable events	Significant events, not observable in practice
a_1=permit CHANGING or DRESSING (an individual reports to the controller on entering)	
	a_2=an individual enters the cabin
	b_2=an individual leaves the cabin
b_1=end CHANGING or DRESSING (an individual reports to the controller on leaving)	

Time

With this notation we have:

$$number\_of\ CABINS\ OCCUPIED = number\_of\ a_2 - number\_of\ b_2$$
$$\leqslant number\_of\ a_1 - number\_of\ b_1$$

If we impose the restriction:

$$number\_of \ a_1 - number\_of \ b_1 \leqslant C$$

then, *a fortiori*, the theoretically required condition

$$number\_of \ a_2 - number\_of \ b_2 \leqslant C$$

holds.

Notice that this situation can be regarded in two different ways.

(i) The first is one in which several abstract expressions are defined. Thus, in our example, one expression (A) would be:

ENTER (a cabin) ;
CHANGE ;
LEAVE (the cabin) ;

which has the precise meaning: 'enter a cabin with a basket in order to change'.

Another expression (B) would be the abstract expression of the action of going into the changing area so as to occupy a cabin and hence to change:

ENTER (changing area) ;
CHANGE ;
LEAVE (changing area) ;

At this level of abstraction, we can then state:

for (A): *number_of CABINS OCCUPIED = number_of ENTER*
− number_of LEAVE

for (B): *number_of CABINS OCCUPIED ≤ number_of ENTER*
− number_of LEAVE

(ii) The second, which is the approach we have adopted, employs only one abstract expression, independent of the events observed. The expression for *CHANGING,* given in section 1.2.1, corresponds to this concept; it assumes that both a basket and a cabin have been acquired and its completion is equated with the release of a basket and a cabin. Given this one expression, we then attempt to introduce the constraints as precisely as possible, in terms of observable quantities.

This second approach is the better one. It makes it possible to envisage various levels of detail in implementation: a very finely tuned implementation is possible for a small swimming pool, where every swimmer can observe the system as a whole — what cabins are free, etc. — and the abstract constraints stated can be satisfied in an optimum manner without any need for a controller.

1.2.5. Distributed control

Suppose now that there are two entrances to the changing area and two controllers $C1$ and $C2$.

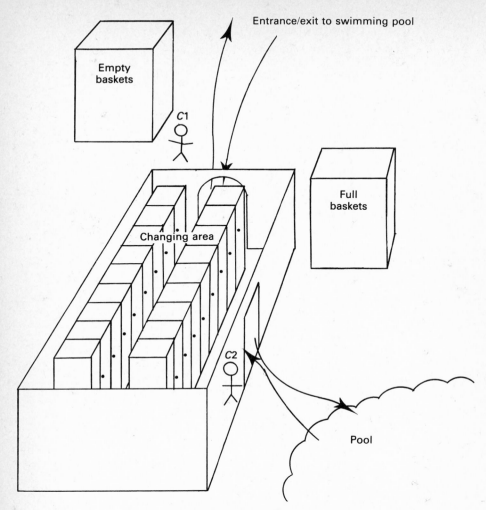

Fig. 4. *A distributed system.*

If both $C1$ and $C2$ are to have an exact knowledge of the number of cabins either occupied or liable to be occupied at any instant, they must communicate their observations and decisions to each other. If they have walkie-talkie radios, they will have no difficulty in ensuring that the abstract constraints already stated are imposed. But suppose that such modern equipment does not exist, or that they have to use a transmission link for which the delay is too long for their purposes, e.g. a runner who goes from $C1$ to $C2$ and back; then, unless further precautions are taken, synchronization constraints cannot be guaranteed. One way to ensure that the system is in control would be for neither controller to allow anyone to enter or to leave the area except when the runner is with him; he would then update his counter and give the value to the runner, who would then run to the other controller, where the process would be repeated. A slight improvement could be made to this method: while the runner was away, the controller could record the probable departures on a private counter, and accept entries against these numbers, updating the common counter only when the runner returned.

We can seek to improve the parallel operation of the two controllers even further by creating an initial stock of C tokens (where C is the number of cabins) and giving them all to $C1$. When a swimmer reports to $C1$, $C1$ cannot allow the swimmer to enter the area unless he, the controller, has at least one token which he can give to the swimmer. The swimmer then changes and gives his token to $C2$ when he passes him on the way to the pool. At the exit from the pool, $C2$ does not allow any swimmer to enter the changing area unless he, $C2$, has at least one token; he gives this to the swimmer, who dresses and gives the token to $C1$ whom he passes on the way out. If, at any instant, $C1$ and $C2$ have c_1 and c_2 tokens respectively, and c_s are held by the swimmers occupying the cabins, then:

$$c_1 + c_2 + c_s = C$$

It could happen that $C1$ had no tokens but $C2$ had a large number; the runner could then be used to rectify the situation by taking a number r, say, of tokens from one to the other.

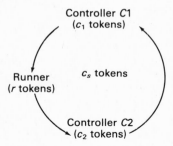

Fig. 5. *Communication using tokens.*

Thus:

$$c_1 + c_2 + c_s + r = C$$

As long as c_s is less than $C-1$, we can expect c_1 and c_2 to remain non-zero, provided that the runner makes his rounds regularly and therefore that the two controllers operate in parallel. The abstract expression for the constraint has remained valid, but its implementation in distributed form has required an *ad hoc* algorithm.

1.2.6. Introduction of priorities

We can refine the control policy at the level of the abstract expression, without changing the text of the processes. In our example, the actions

CHANGING and *DRESSING* are the objects of a request followed by a granting of permission. If, for any action X, we count the number of events *request (X)*, the expression:

number_of request (X) − number_of permit (X) = number_of waiting (X)

gives the number of processes waiting to perform the action X. If we wish to increase the flow of entrants to the pool, we can therefore include a statement that entrants must be given priority for occupation of the cabins, except when there are no more baskets available:

condition for permit *(DRESSING):*
   number_of CHANGING + number_of DRESSING < C
                                   -- at least one cabin free
and *number_of permit (CHANGING) − number_of end (DRESSING) = B*
   or *number_of waiting (CHANGING) = 0*

This suggests that the implementation of a procedure for synchronization involves, among other things, queue management and the establishment of relative priorities among the processes.

1.2.7. Calculations with the abstract expressions

After stating the constraints, the number of baskets occupied can be expressed as the sum of the following terms:

(a) number of cabins occupied:

   number_of permit CHANGING − number_of end CHANGING
     + number_of permit DRESSING − number_of end DRESSING

(b) number of swimmers:

   number_of end CHANGING − number_of request DRESSING

(c) number of people waiting to dress:

   number_of request DRESSING − number_of permit DRESSING

Adding these, we get the expression which we have already found directly:

   number_of permit CHANGING − number_of end DRESSING

The significance of these expressions is not confined to this elementary calculation; they enable important properties of the system to be established, including the impossibility of reaching deadlock or of any process being delayed for an infinite length of time.

IMPOSSIBILITY OF DEADLOCK

A system is said to be in deadlock if there is at least one process waiting and no activity is taking place. We now show that this cannot occur in our example.

Suppose there is at least one process waiting; then:

(1) *number_of waiting CHANGING + number_of waiting DRESSING* ≥ 1

Suppose also that no activity is taking place in the system; then:

(2) *number_of CHANGING = 0*   -- no people are changing
    number_of DRESSING = 0   -- no people are dressing
    number_of end CHANGING − number_of request DRESSING = 0
                                  -- no people are swimming

It follows from (2) that the condition for permission to dress:

number_of CHANGING + number_of DRESSING $< C$

is satisfied, and therefore that:

number_of waiting DRESSING = 0

The number of baskets occupied (the sum of the numbers of people dressing, changing, waiting to dress and swimming) is zero, and therefore the condition for permission to change is also satisfied and:

number_of waiting CHANGING = 0

i.e. *number_of waiting CHANGING + number_of waiting DRESSING = 0*

which contradicts (1), so this situation cannot occur.

IMPOSSIBILITY OF INFINITE WAIT

A process is in a state of infinite wait (starvation) if it is never activated, although the system is not in deadlock. This can result from either of two causes, both of which are considered separately to show that neither can arise in our example.

(a) *Faulty formulation of the problem, leading to a condition for permission that can never be satisfied*

In the swimming pool example, this situation cannot occur: it would result in deadlock since a process must satisfy both permission conditions in order to continue.

Suppose, for example, the condition for permission to dress were false; we should then have the equality *E:*

number_of CHANGING + number_of DRESSING = C

because this sum cannot exceed *C*, the number of cabins.

It follows that the condition for permission to change is not satisfied and therefore the only possible events are:

request CHANGING : this does not affect E; the process is blocked and the activity of the system does not change.

end CHANGING : reduces *number_of CABINS OCCUPIED* by 1, so that, provided that a basket is free, the condition for permission to change is satisfied.

request DRESSING : does not affect E; system activity does not change.

end DRESSING : causes the conditions for permission to dress and to change to become satisfied.

Since the system is not in deadlock, one or other of the events *end DRESSING* or *end CHANGING*, which change the state of activity of the system, will occur within a finite time; the condition for dressing would then be true, contradicting the hypothesis.

(b) *A condition is never considered*

If a condition (A) is always satisfied at the same time as certain other conditions, the processes waiting on these conditions may be privileged and take priority, so that the process waiting on (A) would never be activated. In our example, the condition for permission to change is always satisfied at the same time as that for permission to dress; we shall show that it is impossible for the second condition never to be considered.

The number of active processes is limited by B, the total number of baskets; each process goes successively through the events *permit CHANGING, end CHANGING, permit DRESSING, end DRESSING*. If the condition for permission to change is never considered, the number of active processes will decrease continually and as each process leaves the system it will reduce both the number of occupied baskets and of occupied cabins by 1. After some finite time, all the B processes will have ended their activity and the conditions for permission to change and to dress will both be satisfied. Since there is then no process *waiting DRESSING*, the processes *waiting CHANGING* must be activated, contradicting the hypothesis.

Note: The above proofs of the impossibility of deadlocks or of infinite waits depend upon the abstract expression of the problem, so it is necessary to check that its requirements are preserved in any implementation. In particular, the policies adopted for handling queues of processes must not be such as to invalidate these proofs.

Chapter 2

Abstract expressions in synchronization problems

2.1. Definitions

2.1.1. Order among system events

In the introduction we considered systems of processes, each process consisting of a sequence of events. We shall now study such systems more formally.

Example

Consider a family of processes P_i having actions of two types: LOC_i, involving only objects local to process P_i, and CR_i, involving a common resource R which can be used by only one process at a time, to the exclusion of the others. We therefore have:

Process P_i
cycle
   LOC_i ;
   CR_i
end cycle

The **time trace** of P_i is a word formed from the alphabet $\{LOC_i, CR_i\}$, which can be constructed while P_i is being executed by recording the successive actions; in the example above, the trace has the form $(LOC_i, Cr_i)^*$, where, as usual, $(A)^*$ means zero or more repetitions of A.

We can extend the idea of time trace to the complete system by imagining an external observer able to record every action of the system as it occurs. Since LOC_i and CR_i are of non-zero duration, there may be some overlap of the times — see section 2.1.2. To obtain a precise definition it is convenient to associate with every event A of non-zero duration two fictitious events of zero duration, *start* (A) and *finish* (A). A trace resulting from observation of the system can then take the following form:

$<start(LOC_1)><start(LOC_2)><finish(LOC_1), finish(LOC_2)>$
$<start(CR_1)><finish\ (CR_1)>$

where the notation $<X, Y>$ *means that* X and Y occur at the same instant.

16

Note: Whilst the existence of the time trace of the complete system can be imagined, implying the existence of an idealized external observer, it will be impossible to construct this in the majority of actual cases, at least for systems not having a central clock.

Given the trace resulting from observing a system, we can define two binary relations between pairs of events, denoted by $\twoheadrightarrow$ and $\equiv$:

$A \twoheadrightarrow B$ *iff the date of A is less than or equal to that of B*

$A \equiv B$ *iff the dates of A and B are equal*

Where the 'date' of an event is a measure of some appropriate scale which defines the instant at which the event occurs, $A \twoheadrightarrow B$ means that A occurs before B. The relation $\equiv$ is one of equivalence; $\twoheadrightarrow$ is reflexive and transitive and also has the following property, close to antisymmetry:

$$A \twoheadrightarrow B \ \textbf{and} \ B \twoheadrightarrow A \ \textbf{\textit{implies}} \ A \equiv B$$

With a certain misuse of language, we shall say that the relation $\twoheadrightarrow$ orders a set E (formally, an ordering compatible with $\twoheadrightarrow$ can be constructed on the quotient set $E/\equiv$); it does not give a strict ordering and for that purpose we define the relation:

$$A \rightarrow B \ \textbf{\textit{iff}} \ A \twoheadrightarrow B \ \textbf{and} \ \neg \, (A \equiv B)$$

We must observe the system before we can construct the relation $\twoheadrightarrow$; we then speak of the **resultant ordering** which is not arbitrary but takes into account:

(i) the sequence of events in each process,

(ii) the constraints imposed by synchronization.

Thus, abstractly specifying a synchronization problem consists in expressing prior constraints on the possible resultant orderings. In the above example these constraints are, for example:

$$\forall i,n \ , \ \forall j \neq i \ , \ \exists \, k : start \, (CR_i)^n \twoheadrightarrow start \, (CR_j)^k \rightarrow finish \, (CR_i)^n$$

where A^n is the nth occurrence of event A.

Clearly, only a subset of the events of the system is significant from the point of view of synchronization; we shall call these **sync-points** and denote the subset by E. For the above example,

$$E = \{start \, (CR_i), \, finish \, (CR_i)\}.$$

2.1.2. Partial ordering

We found it necessary to introduce the fictitious instantaneous events *start* (A) and *finish* (A) in order to define the resultant ordering of a system. We can avoid this necessity by defining a strict partial ordering, denoted by $\dashrightarrow$ [Lamport 79]:

$$A \dashrightarrow B \ \textit{iff finish} \ (A) \twoheadrightarrow start \ (B)$$

This expresses the fact that the periods of execution of two events which can be compared in this way do not overlap; events which cannot be thus compared are called **concurrent**.

We could proceed as in section 2.1.1 and say that to specify a synchronization problem is a matter of applying the constraints to the resultant partial ordering of the significant events; so that, for the same example, the specification would be:

$$\forall i,j, \ CR_i \dashrightarrow CR_j \ \textbf{\textit{or}} \ CR_j \dashrightarrow CR_i$$

For example, in [Le Guernic 79], a specification is given in terms of partial ordering for a producer/consumer problem: see also section 4.1.2. This form of expression has the advantage of minimizing the number of events in the set E, although, in some circumstances, fictitious zero duration events have to be included: examples of this will be found in the literature on path expressions [Campbell 74]. On the other hand, in the case of the total orderings defined in section 2.1.1, the specification of constraints on the resultant ordering can be expressed using the time trace. Since this is a work in E^*, it is clear that we can usefully apply formal language theory to these issues. We shall use only the terminology of section 2.1.1 in what follows.

2.1.3. Abstract expression

DEFINITION

We say that the abstract specification of a synchronization problem consists of defining:

(i) the set E of sync-points,

(ii) the language of legitimate time traces, i.e. traces which conform to the time constraints imposed by the synchronization.

PROBLEMS POSED BY SIMULTANEITY

Formally, if $E = \{A_1, A_2, \dots A_N\}$, the alphabet of the language in which the trace is expressed is:

$$V = \{<A_{i_1}, A_{i_2}, \dots A_{i_r}>\}, \text{ where } A_{i_j} \in E \text{ and } 1 \leqslant r \leqslant N$$

because we have admitted the possibility that events can occur simultaneously.

This formalism, however, is clumsy and practically unusable, and we therefore ignore the possibility of simultaneous events. This has no significant consequences. Firstly, whilst two events may occur simultaneously by chance, this cannot be caused to happen: in information science, two events cannot be triggered simultaneously. The closest possible approach is to confine the two occurrences within a very short time interval, such as the basic clock cycle of a computer. Secondly, the circumstances in which simultaneity is required in the specification fall into three classes, for each of which a satisfactory alternative can be specified without using the concept of simultaneity. These are as follows:

(i) **Independence:** it is indifferent to the outcome whichever of these orders is obtained: $A \to B$, $A \equiv B$, $B \to A$. We therefore write $A \to B$ **or** $B \to A$.

(ii) **Precedence:** the order $B \to A$ is forbidden, so either $A \equiv B$ or $A \to B$ is permitted. We therefore write only $A \to B$.

(iii) **Rendezvous:** when simultaneity is required, an equivalent behaviour can be specified by replacing A with a pair of successive events A', A'', with the relations $A' \to B$ and $B \to A''$.

As a consequence of these provisions, we restrict ourselves to languages formed with E^* rather than with V^*.

IMPLEMENTATION

We use the term controller to denote an entity, whether centralized or distributed, which realizes the abstract synchronization expression. A controller observes all those events which are significant as far as synchronization is concerned and it has the means available to delay any process in order to produce a legitimate time trace; in the implementation, the fictitious zero-duration events of E are translated into actions performed by the controller.

For any sync-point A we must identify the following:

— the arrival of a process at this point, signalled by an appeal by the process to the controller which we call a **request**; in general, the controller will record the requests;

— the **permission** given by the controller to the process to continue its execution; this corresponds to the actual point of synchronization;

— the various operations that the controller applies to its internal variables, which may precede or follow this granting of permission.

Consequently, the real events which correspond to those of the abstract expression are permissions, and we may say that a controller has implemented an abstract synchronization expression if the time trace of the permissions is a word in the language which has been defined.

It should be noted, however, that real operating systems, especially distributed systems, have delays due to finite propagation speeds and intermediate processes. These cause the controller's response to requests, and the processes' responses to permissions, to occur later than they would in an ideal system. If the controller is centralized in a single processor, it will be possible to construct the true time trace of the permission. But if it is distributed among several processors which do not have a common clock, we shall have to prove that the union of the time traces (as it might appear to an idealized external observer) of the permissions issued by all the processors conform to the specification. We shall study these two types of control, centralized and distributed, in chapters 3 and 4.

2.1.4. Languages for abstract expression

SYNC-POINTS (SPs)

The choice of these can be either:

(i) left to the programmer, who must then insert them explicitly at appropriate points in the code for each process; failing to do this, or inaccurate handling of SPs, is a source of error,

or:

(ii) partially predetermined by the controller: a number of control procedures are defined and SPs are in effect the calls to and returns from these procedures.

The second option seems, at first sight, to minimize the possibilities for interference between the expression of control and of the controlled processes; however, there is nothing to stop the programmer from providing control procedures with empty bodies and thus, in fact, inserting sync-points explicitly into the process codes.

AUTOMATA

A language on E^* can be defined either by means of a word generator, i.e. a grammar, or by an acceptor, i.e. an automaton. The two methods are equivalent and, because of the evident need to ensure that the implementation is a faithful representation of the specification, the automaton is the means most frequently used.

Defining an automaton is a matter of establishing an association between each sync-point and:

— a record of the request;

— one or more acceptance conditions, which will depend on the state of the automaton's memory;

— the changes to this memory resulting from giving permission to the process to continue from the sync-point.

As an example, consider the swimming-pool problem dealt with in chapter 1. This can be expressed as a finite-state automaton having as many states as there are pairs of elements (number of baskets available, number of cabins available). Transitions are then as shown in Fig. 1.

CLASSIFICATION OF PROBLEMS

The synchronization rules have two complementary objectives for the resolution of problems of competition between processes. It seems useful to distinguish between them:

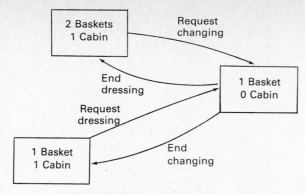

Fig. 1. *Finite-state automaton.*

(i) to ensure that the system operates coherently, meaning that only legal use is made of the resources;

(ii) to ensure either that all processes are treated in the same way (equity), or that a system of ranking is established between them (priority).

In the case of a file which can be used by two classes of processes, readers and writers, objective (i) comes down to ensuring that only one of the writers has access to the file at any one time, whilst (ii) means ensuring, for example, that a group of processes of one class will not prevent use of the file by another class for an indefinite period.

The rules intended to meet the first objective do not, in general, require a knowledge of the identities of blocked processes; those designed with the second objective in mind, whilst they may not need to know actual identities, do at least need to know the classes to which the processes belong, i.e. whether they are readers or writers. So, for example, if there is one writer waiting for the file, every new request from a reader must be made to wait until the writer's request has been dealt with.

It follows that it is the automaton that represents the rules concerned with the second of the above objectives which has the greater need for memory facilities. Some control languages make explicit use of process queues and are therefore particularly well adapted to dealing with the expression of equity or priority. We give two examples in section 2.3, whilst in section 2.2 we develop methods which, though in general less powerful, are adequate for dealing with most problems concerning the coherence of a system.

2.2. Examples of languages for abstract expression

We shall study four methods which have been proposed for the abstract expression of synchronization:

(i) **synchronization controllers** [Pulou 78],

(ii) **synchronization words** [Roucairol 78],

(iii) **control modules** [Robert 77],

(iv) **path expressions** [Campbell 74, Habermann 75].

The information in the controller's memory concerning the past history of the system must be sufficient either to permit or to defer passage through the sync-points. We have seen that this history may be condensed to a greater or lesser extent; a compromise has to be found between:

— leaving it to the programmer to decide the data structures to be used by the controller; this enables any problem to be tackled but is a potential source of error and impairs the readability of the programs;

— restricting the data structures to a limited number of types (e.g. finite number of states, counters, queues, etc.), which makes the controller easier to understand but reduces its power.

Our preference is for the second choice, since the loss of power involved seems minimal. Consequently, a finite-state automaton, even with its limited memory facilities, is powerful enough to deal with the majority of synchronization problems because all that is necessary is that the number of processes to be controlled and the number of resources should be finite. However, it is difficult to give objective criteria, and the choice of any particular tool will depend above all on the circumstances in which it is to be used, e.g. on the extent to which the past history of the system in question has to be taken into account. In the following sections we discuss the above four methods, in an order selected for the sake of clarity rather than for any other reason.

2.2.1. Synchronization controllers

The method proposed by Pulou [Pulou 78] requires the programmer to locate the sync-points explicitly in the process code; he also defines and initializes the state variables. The controller uses these variables and may also have access to some of the program variables. The behaviour of the automaton is then specified completely when an association has been established between each sync-point and:

— a condition to be fulfilled before passage through the point is allowed: this is a predicate involving the controller's state variables and possibly some of the program variables too;

— the rules giving the transformations of the state variable when any sync-point is passed.

Example 1

Consider a family of cyclic processes which use a resource R via a procedure $UTILIZATION$; R has N entry points, where N is a constant. The controller can have the following form:

sync-points *STRTU, FINU ;*   *co* at the start and finish respectively of
                                       UTILIZATION co

*integer variable NUTI **initialized to** 0 ;*
*STRTU ⟷ **condition** NUTI < N*
            ***transformation** NUTI := NUTI + 1 ;*
*FINU ⟷ **condition true***
         ***transformation** NUTI := NUTI − 1 ;*

Example 2

If we turn again to the swimming-pool problem, in section 1.2, the process code is:

```
begin SC ;
      CHANGING ;
      FC ;
      SWIMMING ;
      SD ;
      DRESSING ;
      FD ;
  end
```

and the controller is:

sync-points SC, FC, SD, FD ;
*variables NBRCABOCC **initialized to** 0 ;*
        *NBRBASOCC **initialized to** 0 ;*

*SC ⟷ **condition** NBRCABOCC < C **and** NBRBASOCC < B*
      ***transformation** NBRCABOCC := NBRCABOCC + 1 ;*
                NBRBASOCC := NBRBASOCC + 1 ;

*FC ⟷ **condition true***
      ***transformation** NBRCABOCC := NBRCABOCC − 1 ;*

*SD ⟷ **condition** NBRCABOCC < C*
      ***transformation** NBRCABOCC := NBRCABOCC + 1 ;*

*FD ⟷ **condition true***
      ***transformation** NBRCABOCC := NBRCABOCC − 1 ;*
                NBRBASOCC := NBRBASOCC − 1 ;

This illustrates the simplicity of the expression for the controller. The conditions for continuing from the sync-points *SC* and *SD* are an exact translation of the invariant for the problem (see section 1.2.2).

We must, however, point out that there is some danger in the freedom given to the programmer in choosing variables; in this case, for example, he could have decided to count occupied cabins separately for those entering the site and for those leaving, which would have been an unnecessary complication. There are similar dangers in the freedom to locate the sync-points, quite apart from the interference between the programming of processes and their control: a choice could be, for example, to have separate sync-points for acquiring cabins and acquiring baskets, which could lead to deadlock.

The freedom to choose the state variables for the controller puts no restriction on the complexity of the language generated by the trace of the sync-point crossings, and in this sense this expression is very general. However, proofs concerning the behaviour of the controller could be difficult to establish, and so the proposals we consider next do impose some limitations on this choice.

2.2.2. Synchronization words

In [Roucairol 78], the controller's state variables are words, called **synchronization words**, formed from an arbitrary alphabet. Passing a sync-point now involves some sequence of operations on these words, the possible operations being the following:

— addition of a letter at the head of the word: *APPEND*,

— deletion of the first occurrence, starting from the head, of a letter from the word: *DELETE*,

— halting the process until particular letters appear at the heads of particular words and possibly modifying these words: *TEST DELETE, TEST APPEND*.

Example 3: acquisition of a resource which has N entry points.

— The alphabet here consists of a single letter, r say, and there is only one synchronization word M, initialized to r^N.

— The procedure *UTILIZATION* is preceded by *TEST(M:r) DELETE (M:r)*, which halts the process until the letter r appears at the head of word M; when this happens, this letter is deleted and the procedure *UTILIZATION* entered. At the end of the procedure *UTILIZATION*, the action *APPEND(M:r)* is performed.

Example 4: the swimming-pool problem once more.

Here, the alphabet is again the single letter r, and the synchronization words are: *BAS* initialized to r^B, *CAB* initialized to r^C.

The sync-points are:

before CHANGING : *TEST(BAS:r,CAB:r) DELETE(BAS:r,CAB:r)*
after CHANGING : *APPEND(CAB:r)*
before DRESSING : *TEST(CAB:r) DELETE(CAB:r)*
after DRESSING : *APPEND(CAB:r,BAS:r)*

In examples 3 and 4, the synchronization words are used simply to count the events, and a single-letter alphabet will always suffice for such a purpose. The two solutions are very similar to those of examples 1 and 2, with the same advantages and disadvantages.

2.2.3. Control modules

In [Robert 77], the choice of sync-points is not left to the programmer; access to resources or shared variables is gained by means of access procedures, with each of which are associated three particular events: request, permission and termination, corresponding respectively to a call by the process to the access procedure, the start of the access (under control of the automaton) and its completion.

For each procedure P, the controller maintains the state variables:

$$\# \ req \ (P), \ \# \ perm \ (P), \ \# \ term \ (P)$$

which record the numbers of requests, permissions and terminations, respectively, associated with P since the initialization of the system. These variables are called **counters** and it is convenient to add another two:

$$\# \ exec \ (P) \ = \ \# \ perm \ (P) \ - \ \# \ term \ (P)$$

$$\# \ wait \ (P) \ = \ \# \ req \ (P) \ - \ \# \ perm \ (P)$$

giving the number of processes executing P and the number waiting for permission to execute P, respectively.

Changes to the state variables are made according to the way the processes develop and are represented by the updates of the counters; the only sync-point subject to an *a priori* condition is that of permission, and this condition is expressed by a predicate involving the control module counters.

Example 5: for access to a resource having N entry points.

$$condition \ (UTILIZATION) \ = \ \# \ exec \ (UTILIZATION) \ < \ N$$

Example 6: the swimming-pool problem.

$$condition \ (CHANGING) \ = \ \# \ exec \ (CHANGING)$$
$$+ \ \# \ exec \ (DRESSING) \ < \ C$$
$$\textbf{\textit{and}} \quad \# \ perm \ (CHANGING)$$
$$- \ \# \ term \ (DRESSING) \ < \ B$$

$$condition \ (DRESSING) \ = \ \# \ exec \ (CHANGING)$$
$$+ \ \# \ exec \ (DRESSING) \ < \ C$$

This may seem a less natural method than that of synchronization controllers because it involves considering the state of the processes rather than that of the resource. The two methods are, however, complementary and any restriction imposed by the control module method is compensated by a greater separation between control expression and processing expression.

As far as the descriptive power of the language is concerned, it is clear that some items of information — such as the identities of the processes — cannot be recorded in counters. We shall return to this point in section 2.3, where we give a problem which cannot be treated in this way, and propose some extensions to the method.

2.2.4. Control expression by means of regular language

A controller can be defined by means of a finite-state automaton. Thus, for a resource having N entry points, we can choose $N + 1$ states numbered 0 to N, where state i corresponds to that of the system in which i entry points to the resource are available. If, as before (section 2.2.1), we write *STRTU, FINU* for the start and finish of use of the resource, we can define an automaton whose principal behaviour is as follows:

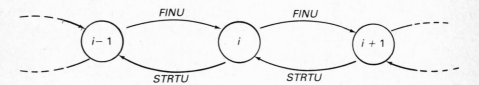

The solution of the swimming-pool problem, in terms of regular languages, is sketched at the beginning of section 2.1.4.

The limit to the power of such representation is set by the target language. Regular languages can deal with most practical cases, because a resource usually has only a finite number of entry points and, therefore, can be represented by a finite-state automaton, but the clarity of the resulting expressions suffers as the number of states becomes large.

The main merit of this form of representation is that it lends itself easily to the development of proofs of system behaviour, whether by automatic methods or otherwise; we give an informal example later in this section. Finally, regular expressions are strictly equivalent to finite-state automata, and their use to specify synchronization is a subset of Campbell's **path expressions** [Campbell 74], a concept we now explain briefly.

PATH EXPRESSIONS

The language of path expressions uses the following names of procedures and operators:

(i) **Sequentiality:**   the expression $P;Q$ states that procedure Q cannot start unless P has been completed.

(ii) **Selection:**   the expression P,Q states that only one of the two procedures P and Q can be executed.

(iii) **Iteration:**   the expression ***path e end*** states that the time-dependent relations specified by the expression e can be repeated indefinitely: e could be, for example, $P;Q$ or $(P,Q);R$.

(iv) **Simultaneity:** a simultaneity operator has been introduced in order to make it possible to allow certain events which affect the synchronization to take place in parallel. It is difficult to give this a non-operational semantics, and its general usefulness is debatable.

$\{P\}$ is used to indicate that a number of parallel executions of the procedure P are allowed; this can be extended to $\{e\}$ where e is a path expression, indicating the parallel operation of an indefinite number of controllers, any one of which can respond to the expression e.

More details of this method will be found in [Lauer 75, Flon 76], which give, in particular, extensions for dealing with problems of priorities.

ANALYSIS USING A REGULAR LANGUAGE

We give now an informal example to illustrate the techniques of semi-automatic analysis which can be applied to synchronization rules expressed in the form of a finite-state automaton.

One of the possible analyses of the swimming-pool problem leads to the definition of just four sync-points: acquiring and releasing a cabin (*ACQCAB*, *RELCAB*) and acquiring and releasing a basket (*ACQBAS*, *RELBAS*). With a stock of one cabin and two baskets, we can represent the controller by an automaton A as follows:

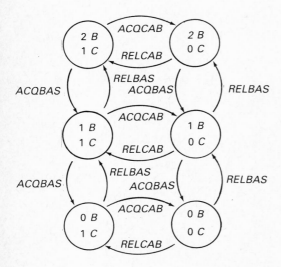

The process code is as follows:

```
begin
  cycle
  ACQCAB ;
  ACQBAS ;
  CHANGING ;
  RELCAB ;
  SWIMMING ;
  ACQCAB ;
  DRESSING ;
  RELCAB ;
  RELBAS ;
  endcycle
end
```

The following automaton can be used to represent the passage of a process through its sync-points:

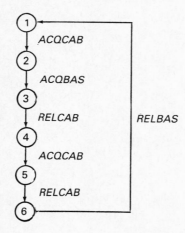

Consider now three processes $P1$, $P2$ and $P3$. Deadlock can occur if there is neither a free cabin nor a free basket, i.e. if the state of A is $(0B, 0C)$, and only requests are being made, e.g.:

P1 is in state 4: has 1 basket, requests 1 cabin
P2 is in state 4: has 1 basket, requests 1 cabin
P3 is in state 2: has 1 cabin, requests 1 basket

In practice, the blocking states can be detected by means of an automaton $\mathcal{A}$ which describes the working of the system as a whole; this is constructed by merging the separate automata for $P1$, $P2$ and $P3$ and then merging the result with A, the operation of merging being defined informally as giving all possible combinations of the actions of the separate processes. The blocking states are those states of $\mathcal{A}$ in which no transition is possible.

A related analytical technique is that of constructing the Petri net for the operations on the resources and simulating the evolution of the processes on this net; the nets for the swimming-pool problem and for the deadlock situation are given in [Latteux 80]. The techniques for validation of protocols and the theory of finite-state automata are also applicable [West 77].

2.3. Priority problems

2.3.1. Introduction

Equity or non-equity (i.e. priority) are issues that enter into the abstract expression of a synchronization problem. For example, where access to a critical resource is concerned we could make either of these rules:

When two processes $P1$ and $P2$ are both waiting for access to the resource:

either   (1) $P1$ must always be given access: this gives $P1$ priority,
or   (2) access must always be given to the one which has been waiting longest: this is one way of ensuring equity.

In order to make a decision, therefore, the automaton must always know the identities of the processes which have requested but not been granted access, or the class to which these processes belong. Of the methods described in section 2.2, only the approach based on synchronization controllers and synchronization words provides such storage in full generality; the others — control modules and path expressions — require extensions before they can meet this need (see, for example [Verjus 78; Flon 76]).

A representation of those processes which have requested access to a resource but have not yet been granted access is called a **queue**. In problems where priorities change with time, several queues have to be maintained, through which the processes progress; and if the synchronization controller method is used, sync-points must be inserted at each passage of a process from one queue to another, leading to interference between the expressions for control and for processing.

Later in this section, we shall explain two means by which complex priority rules can be programmed within the controller without encroaching on the process code: serializers [Hewitt 79] and extended control modules [Verjus 78]. We shall illustrate both by means of the example in section 2.3.2 below.

2.3.2. Example of synchronization with priorities [Hoare 74]

We consider the use of a common file F by two classes of processes: readers R, using a procedure $READ$, and writers W, using a procedure $WRITE$. We wish to frame synchronization rules which will take into account:

(i) the logic of access to the data held in F: several readers can be allowed concurrent access, but only one writer may be given access at any one time. This is rule R1;

(ii) equity considerations: it should not be possible for a coalition of members of either class to be formed so as to deny access by other processes indefinitely.

Also, we have the following rules [Hoare 74]:

R2(1): A reader arriving when other readers are using the file is made to wait if there is at least one writer waiting.

R2(2): When a *WRITE* access terminates, all the waiting readers are given access.

Rule R1 can be enforced by a controller if it has two queues, one (*R*) for readers and one (*W*) for writers. The system is summarized in Fig. 2.

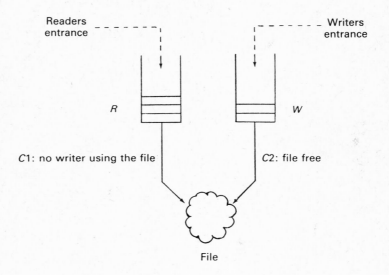

Fig. 2. *Readers/writers without priority.*

Let *C*1 be the condition which must be satisfied if the reader at the head of its queue is allowed to leave the queue and use the file, and *C*2 the corresponding condition for a writer; these are:

*C*1: no writer using the file.

*C*2: file free (i.e. neither reader nor writer using it).

Starting from this model, the priority rules R2 can be included. A natural way to do this is to introduce a new queue *A*, effectively a waiting-room, in which readers are placed as they arrive. By rule R2(1), they are queued in *A* if a writer is waiting, and by rule R2(2), if a writer is using the file all those in *A* are transferred to *R* where they are given priority over writers. The condition *C*3 that now has to be satisfied if a reader at the head of queue *A* is to be allowed to transfer to *R* is:

*C*3: *W* is empty (i.e. no writer waiting) or a writer is using *F*

The new system is shown in Fig. 3.

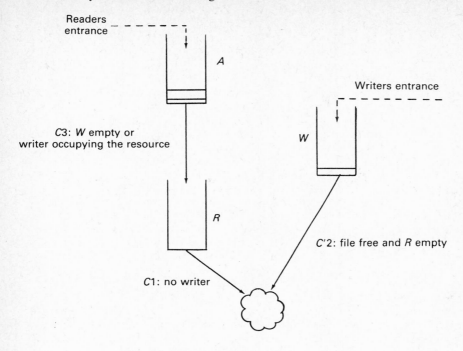

Fig. 3. *Hoare's problem.*

A controller operating according to these rules can be defined provided that the following can be specified:

— an arbitrary number of queues,

— the conditions to be satisfied for the transfer of a process from one queue to another; these will be predicates in the states of the queues and the resource.

The methods described in sections 2.3.3 and 2.3.4 have these features.

Note: In the above example, each queue contains only one class of process; if this is not the case, the transition rules may vary according to the class of process at the head of the queue. The reader/writer problem could, for example, be processed according to the order in which requests arrive and could be programmed with a single general file *GEN* as shown in Fig. 4.

2.3.3. Serializers

This concept is due to Hewitt [Hewitt 79], who developed it in connection with his actor model [Hewitt 77]. In the interests of ease of reading, we give an account of it using the syntax developed by Le Guernic [Le Guernic 79].

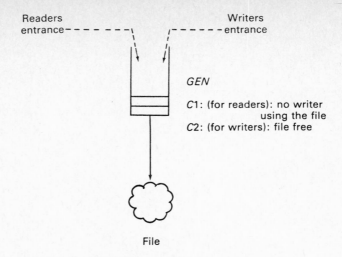

Fig. 4. *Readers/writers by order of arrival.*

A serializer is an automaton for which the significant events are calls by the processes to certain procedures which we call controlled procedures. Variables of any type can be declared in a serializer, but two types are of particular importance: the **queues**, and the **journals** in which the state of occupation of the resource is recorded.

At each procedure call, the serializer causes the calling process to pass through one of a succession of queues and on leaving the last queue it enters one of the journals, where it remains during execution of the procedure; the process leaves the serializer when this execution terminates.

A serializer is programmed by describing the progress of each process through the queues by means of statements of the form:

— *wait in QUEUE leave when CONDITION*, which places the process in the queue named *QUEUE*, from which it passes when *CONDITION* is true. *CONDITION* is a predicate on the variables defining the state of the serializer's memory, i.e. which of the queues and logs are empty, and the states of other variables;

— *through JOURNAL*, which gives permission for the procedure to be executed.

A sequence of statements such as:

wait in F1 leave when C1 ;

wait in F2 ...

therefore means that the process concerned cannot pass from *F1* to *F2* until condition *C1* is satisfied.

Applying the method to Hoare's problem (section 2.3.2, Fig. 2), we have the following solution:

queues A, R, W ;
journals READ, WRITE
for READ = co progress of readers co
   wait in *A* **leave when empty** *(W)* **or** ⌐ **empty** *(WRITE) ;*
   wait in *R* **leave when empty** *(WRITE)* **through** *READ ;*
for WRITE = co progress of writers co
   wait in W **leave when empty** *(WRITE)* **and empty** *(READ)* **and empty** *(R)*
   'through WRITE ;

2.3.4. Extended control modules

Control modules were explained in section 2.2.3; the extension enables them to be used for the passage of processes through queues [Verjus 78].

We specify a controller by declaring a number of queues together with conditions of the general form:

   condition (SOURCE QUEUE, P, DESTINATION) = $\mathcal{P}$

where *SOURCE QUEUE* is a queue associated with one or more procedures; *P* gives the class of the process at the head of the queue, as defined by the procedure that it calls. This parameter can be omitted if all the processes in the queue are to be treated in the same way; *DESTINATION* is a queue in which the process waits until the condition is satisfied. If this is omitted the process which leaves *SOURCE QUEUE* is allowed to execute; and $\mathcal{P}$ is a predicate depending on the following counters:

   # perm(PROC)
   # term(PROC)
   # exec(PROC)   see section 2.2
   # req(PROC)
   # wait(PROC)
   # req waiting(QUEUE)
   # req waiting(QUEUE, PROC)

The solution to Hoare's problem can now be written:

queues A, R, W
for READ enter A ;
for WRITE enter W ;
condition (A, READ, R) = *# req waiting(W) = 0* **or** *# exec(WRITE) = 1*
condition (R, READ) = *# exec(WRITE) = 0*
condition (W, WRITE) = *# exec(WRITE) = 0* **and** *# exec(READ) = 0*
                         and *# req waiting(R) = 0*

Chapter 3

Centralized implementation

3.1. Introduction

Implementing the solution to a synchronization problem consists in defining an operational mechanism which conforms to the requirements of the specification, i.e. of the abstract expression which has been constructed for the problem. Most of the abstract expressions described in section 2.2 define:

— a set of variables, representing the states of the processes and/or the resources,

— a set of conditions, functions of the state variables, which determine the way in which the processes evolve,

— the changes that are to be made to the state variables in the course of this evolution.

Behind these expressions is the assumption that all operations on the variables are coherent, i.e. those that are applied at each synchronization event can be regarded as instantaneous. Consequently, the implementation must specify:

(i) the details of the representation chosen for the variables, such as their location and the number of copies of each,

(ii) the details of the representation chosen for the operations, i.e. of the programs which perform them,

(iii) the way in which the programs are to be executed.

Action (iii) must ensure that the required coherence is respected: since the execution time for the sequences of statements associated with the sync-point is not in fact negligible, there can be mutual interference between sequences if precautions are not taken to prevent it.

The implementations can be grouped into two classes according to the representation chosen for the variables: **centralized**, in which all the variables are held in a single memory and there is only one copy of each; and **distributed**, in which the variables are shared and distributed in a variety of ways. Centralized systems are dealt with in this chapter and distributed systems in chapter 4.

3.2. Systems with common memory

3.2.1. Characteristics of common-memory systems

We assume that the architectural framework within which we are working has the following features:

— there are one or more processes sharing a **single central memory,**

— only one processor can access this memory at any one moment, and the access operation, which can be either for reading or for writing, is **atomic** (i.e. once started it must run to completion).

These properties are used in constructing what we have called a centralized implementation, as follows:

(i) Each variable exists only as **a single copy** in the central memory, where it is potentially accessible to any process running on any processor in the system;

(ii) a means for **mutual exclusion** between different sequences of statements seeking to access the same variable can easily be provided. Algorithms such as those given by Dijkstra [Dijkstra 68] effect this by using the atomic property of read/write operations; alternatively, statements such as 'Test And Set' are available with several processors, by means of which the exclusion can be programmed more directly.

Feature (ii) can be used to express the indivisibility of the sequences associated with the sync-points, and thus provides a relatively simple way of ensuring the coherence of the operations. However, it must be remembered that, in contrast to the assumed idealized 'execution' of the abstract expression, statement sequences put into a state of mutual exclusion may occupy a non-negligible amount of time; this slows down the running of the system because processes may have to remain blocked for long periods before being given access to the memory.

We shall see in the next section that it is not always necessary to impose this mutual exclusion on all the operations in order to ensure the coherence of the state variables. Processes can be allowed to execute in parallel and at their own rates, provided that they respect the synchronization constraints and the requirements for the elementary read/write operations to be atomic.

3.2.2. Choice of state variables

The following example shows that, according to the choice of variables to be held in memory, the operations corresponding to the synchronization requirements need or need not be performed (partially or wholly) in a mutually exclusive manner in order to remain coherent. The example illustrates several properties of the variables and of the operations which enable the necessary extent of the exclusion to be determined.

PRODUCER–CONSUMER PROBLEM

We consider a pair of processes, one of which, the **producer**, sends messages to the other, the **consumer**. Messages which have been produced but not consumed are held in N buffers, used cyclically; a buffer becomes available for use again when its message has been consumed.

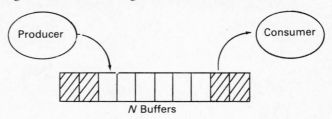

Fig. 1. *Producer/consumer problem.*

In terms of control modules (section 2.2.3), the following is an abstract expression for the problem:

condition *(produce): # perm (produce)* − *# term (consume)* < *N*
condition *(consume): # term (produce)* − *# perm (consume)* > *0*

We shall now suggest two possible implementations.

METHOD 1: USE OF PROCESS STATES

This consists of an exact translation of the abstract expression, representing the evolution of the processes by four variables corresponding to the four counters used in the specification:

start production	representing *# perm (produce)*,
finish production	representing *# term (produce)*,
start consumption	representing *# perm (consume)*,
finish consumption	representing *# term (consume)*,

The processes can be expressed as follows (we have paid more attention to the accesses to the variables than to the programming style):

process *producer:*
   wait *start production* − *finish consumption* < *N* ;
   start production := *start consumption* + *1* ;
      produce ;
   finish production := *finish production* + *1* ;
end *producer* ;
process *consumer* ;
   wait *finish production* − *start consumption* > *0* ;
   start consumption := *start consumption* + *1* ;
      consume ;

finish consumption := *finish consumption* + 1 ;
end *consumer* ;

Note: wait corresponds to a loop which is executed while the condition is not satisfied — the 'active wait'.

This expression ensures coherence among the processes without the state variables having to be updated entirely via mutually exclusive operations. If the producer is testing the condition for *produce* at the same time as the consumer is updating the variable *finish consumption*, only the access to this variable need be atomic — as will be ensured automatically by the machine architecture — and not the associated operations of testing and modifying. At worst, the variable *finish consumption* would contain the value that it had before the modification was completed, with the result that the next production would be delayed.

It is sufficient for coherence if the elementary read/write access operations are atomic, for then:

(i) only one process can modify a given variable at any one time,

(ii) the solution is not invalidated by the reading of an 'old' value because the variables are monotonic; in this example, they only increase as the process evolves, they never decrease.

METHOD 2: USE OF RESOURCE STATES

The 'resource' here is the set of buffers, of which the state can be represented by two variables, *number_of filled* and *number_of empty*, initialized to 0 and N respectively. This is equivalent to a change of variables in Method 1, as follows:

number_of filled = *finish production* − *start consumption*
number_of empty = *N* + *finish consumption* − *start production*

The processes are now as follows:

process *producer* :
  wait *number_of empty* > 0 ;
  number_of empty := *number_of empty* − 1 ;
    produce ;
  number_of full := *number_of full* + 1 ;
end *producer* ;
process *consumer* :
  wait *number_of full* > 0 ;
  number_of full := *number_of full* − 1 ;
    consume ;
  number_of empty := *number_of empty* + 1 ;
end *consumer* ;

This is coherent only if the following operations are made mutually exclusive:

$$\begin{cases} number\_of \ empty := number\_of \ empty + 1 \\ number\_of \ empty := number\_of \ empty - 1 \end{cases}$$

and similarly for *number_of full*. To ensure coherence, therefore, the two processes must be modified by the insertion of requests for this exclusive use, before operations for which it is needed, and for its removal afterwards.

CONCLUSION

In this second implementation, the extent to which the two processes can run independently is limited:

(i) by the logical constraints of the synchronization: they must wait until conditions embodied in the abstract expression are satisfied;

(ii) by constraints imposed by the implementation itself: exclusive use has to be gained by all the sequences which read and modify the same variable.

Nevertheless, the producer–consumer problem is often implemented in this way, which, because it requires only two variables to be managed, seems the more natural and the simpler. A deeper analysis of the problem, made without any assumption of a form of implementation, shows that a solution can be found which is more efficient and closer to the logical requirements. Furthermore, we shall show in chapter 4 that the asynchronous behaviour of the two processes, which is preserved by the first method, can be used to provide an implementation on a distributed system. We shall then consider again those properties of variables and expressions which make the use of mutual exclusion advantageous.

3.3. Implementation techniques

We continue on the assumption that we are dealing only with centralized systems. Given that the analysis of the problem has been completed and the choice of variables and their representation has been made, there are still two choices to be made: the form of the control statements and the way in which they are to be executed. There are two ways of programming control statements:

(a) they can all be grouped together in a single entity; this preserves the structure of the abstract expression, which is then separated from the text of the cooperating processes;

(b) they can be located in the process texts as required, at the places corresponding to the sync-points.

As far as mode of execution is concerned, several methods can be used if choice (a) has been made, of which the extremes are:

(1) all the control statements are executed by a single process when it is called by an application process,

(2) each application process itself executes the control statements in the form of a procedure call.

Intermediate choices can be envisaged: for example, the procedures called directly by the application processes could themselves call 'servers' for certain actions.

If choice (b) is made, this implies that the application processes execute control statements.

The possibilities are summarized in the table below.

Programming Execution	Grouped statements (a)	Scattered statements (b)
n processes + 1 special process (1)	interpreter	—
n processes (2)	sharable module	shared variables

We shall now study these possibilities in more detail, showing what primitive statements are needed in each case.

3.3.1. Interpreter for the control statements

The declarations of all the state variables, and all the statements which act on them, are grouped together in a single entity or module in a form corresponding to the abstract expression. These statements are executed by a single process which is called by the cooperating processes when they are at sync-points. This special process is the controller, which acts as an accepter for a language defined by the synchronization events; it can only execute one control operation at a time, and it is this which ensures that its operations are atomic. On the other hand, there must be mutual exclusion between the calls made to the controller by the application processes, which will usually be in the form of messages, of which only one at a time will be accepted by the controller. This can be realized, for example, using a data structure of the 'mail-box' type, to which the processes have mutually exclusive access: when any process has placed a message in the box, it must wait until the controller allows it to continue.

The primitives which are of help in writing an interpreter for the control statements therefore have the following functions:

(a) **Message sending**: this is used by the cooperating processes and **causes them to be blocked.**

(b) **Process restart**: this is used by the controller after it has dealt with the message from a process, provided that the conditions under which the process may resume are satisfied.

A process may be blocked for a shorter or longer period, according to the evaluation of the conditions for its resumption. When the values of the state variables have changed, the controller must re-examine the conditions associated with blocked processes, or at least those which may have been modified as a consequence of the state changes.

3.3.2. Shared modules

Syntactically, this is similar to the above method. All the control variables and procedures are gathered together in a single module and are called as necessary by the cooperating processes; these calls replace the previous sending of messages to the controller. However, there is now the possibility of several procedures being executed in parallel and, therefore, a mutual exclusion must be imposed when several procedures wish to access the same variables. Furthermore, when executing procedures, a process must block itself if the condition for its continuation is not satisfied; operations must also be implemented for the release of blocked processes.

The relevant primitives here are:

(a) **Procedure call:** this is a call to a single procedure in the module, which runs in 'mutual' exclusion; this ensures atomic operation.

(b) **Process block:** if, during execution of a control procedure, the process concerned finds that a condition for its continuation is not satisfied, it must block itself and remove the exclusion imposed on the module.

(c) **Procedure return:** the exclusion is removed when a control procedure ends.

(d) **Process release:** usually, when there are changes in the state variables, the conditions for the release of blocked processes are re-evaluated and those for which the conditions are satisfied are allowed to resume. One of the major problems of this method arises here: the release of the processes must not compromise the mutual exclusion. The processes which have been released must therefore run one after the other and without interference with the process which has released them.

To avoid the problem described in (d), the primitive for releasing a process may be made unavailable to the programmer; releasing then occurs automatically when the mutual exclusion is removed. Every process which has been released must then check that the condition for its resumption is satisfied, otherwise it must block itself again.

3.3.3. Shared variables

In this method the variables are manipulated directly by the processes themselves, the control statements being located at the sync-points in the relevant programs; only those statements that are necessary to a particular point are given at that point. If a number of points are equivalent, the statements are copied as many times as is necessary. As in the above method, the processes can execute in parallel, and mutual exclusion must be programmed so that any desirable indivisibility of the control operations is ensured; but, in this case, the exclusion can act on any sequence of statements whatsoever and not only on complete procedures. Apart from the exclusion, operations for blocking and releasing processes are usually available.

The primitives in this case are the following:

(a) **Mutual exclusion:** two operations are needed, to enter and leave a sequence of statements, respectively, excluding all others.

(b) **Process block:** to halt a process and release the exclusion.

(c) **Process release:** there are two types of release primitive: those which release only those processes for which the conditions for resumption are now found to be satisfied, and those which release all the blocked processes, leaving it to each of these to check that its own conditions for resumption are satisfied (cf. section 3.3.2).

3.3.4. Conclusion

Whatever method of solution is adopted, some means for imposing mutual exclusion must be provided if the method is to be applicable to all synchronization problems — although, as we saw in section 3.2.2, there are synchronization problems for which this is not needed — and this exclusion can apply to messages left in a mail-box, to complete processes or to arbitrary sequences of statements. In section 3.5, we shall study three mechanisms for achieving this exclusion which provide primitives well adapted to the needs of the three methods we have just described; but first, in section 3.4, we shall describe a basic tool, the semaphore, which can be used to express mutual exclusion and with the aid of which all methods for solving synchronization problems can be programmed.

3.4. Basic tools for mutual exclusion: semaphores
3.4.1. Definition

Semaphores, and primitives P and V associated with them [Dijkstra 68], provide a basis for the study of synchronization mechanisms.

A semaphore S is a data structure consisting of a counter s which takes integer values and a queue q which is initially empty; the initial value of s can be positive or zero. The operations P and V are defined as follows:

$P(S)$: $s := s - 1$;
    if $s < 0$ **then** put the process in the queue q **endif** ;
$V(S)$: $s := s + 1$;
    if $s \leqslant 0$ **then** activate a process held in the queue q **endif** ;

These primitives are **atomic**, guaranteeing that the conditional statement and the associated operations are always executed consecutively.

A process executing *P(S)* can find itself blocked if *s* is negative or zero, when only a *V(S)* operation can release it. If *s* is negative, its absolute value gives the number of blocked processes; if it is positive, it gives the maximum possible number of simultaneous executions.

A sequence of statements to execute to the exclusion of all others, what we call a **critical section** *CS* of the program, can be programmed as follows. A semaphore *MUTEX* is declared with initial value 1, to represent the maximum number of simultaneous executions of *CS*. A process must perform *P(MUTEX)* before any execution of *CS* and it will be blocked if *CS* is already being executed; *V(MUTEX)* is called when *CS* ends, possibly allowing a blocked process to resume and thus enter the critical section.

The semaphore makes it possible to implement synchronization expressions in a centralized environment. Access to the synchronization variables or to the controller is protected by defining a semaphore for each variable or group of variables and for the controller, and the processes execute the primitives *P* and *V*, respectively, before and after each synchronization procedure. The semaphores themselves can be used to represent the synchronization variables directly; these will then be summarized in counters taking values which are positive or zero, with processes being blocked when values are zero.

3.4.2. Examples of use of semaphores

We return to the swimming-pool problem of section 1.2 and consider the expression for procedure *changing*, with its associated synchronization conditions (cf. section 2.2.3):

condition (changing) = # *exec (changing)* + # *exec (dressing)* < C
and # *perm (changing)* − # *term (dressing)* < B

We show two ways in which semaphores can be used to program this procedure.

METHOD 1: MUTUALLY EXCLUSIVE CONTROL SEQUENCES

Here, the control statements can either be included in the cooperating processes or form the procedures of a module; in either case, they all execute in a mutually exclusive manner.

We define a variable for each counter used in the synchronization expressions and a semaphore *mutex* to bring about the mutual exclusion. The following statements correspond to the procedure *changing*:

start CHANGING : P(MUTEX) ;
if number_of CHANGING
+ number_of DRESSING < C
and *number_of permit CHANGING*
− number_of end DRESSING < B

> **then** *number_of CHANGING*
>   := *number_of CHANGING + 1 ;*
>   *number_of permit CHANGING*
>   := *number_of permit CHANGING + 1 ;*
>   *V(MUTEX)*
> **else** *V(MUTEX) ;*
>   **goto** *start CHANGING*
> **endif** *;*
>   ...

Notice that waiting for the condition to be satisfied is programmed as an 'active wait' (loop), during which the mutual exclusion has to be lifted.

This form follows exactly the abstract expression but is cumbersome and results in an inefficient execution.

METHOD 2: SEMAPHORE REPRESENTATION OF THE RESOURCE STATE

If we make the change of variables:

number_of cabins free = C − # exec (changing) − # exec (dressing)
number_of baskets free = B − # perm (changing) + # term (dressing)

the condition for *dressing* becomes:

condition (dressing) = number_of cabins free > 0
                              and *number_of baskets free > 0*

We can implement this by defining two semaphores, *number_of cabins free* and *number_of baskets free*, initialized respectively to their maxima C and B and reduced by 1 at every acquisition; the requests made by the processes are blocked when the values are zero or negative. The start of the procedure *changing* thus corresponds to '*get a basket and a cabin*', and the program is:

(1)   *P(number_of baskets free) ;*
(2)   *P(number_of cabins free) ;*
        ...

These operations, however, do not correspond exactly to the condition for *changing*, given above, and in fact it would be better to operate **simultaneously** on the two semaphores.

The inverse sequence:

(2)   *P(number_of cabins free) ;*
(1)   *P(number_of baskets free) ;*
        ...

can lead to deadlock. If B people are in the pool, *number_of baskets free* is zero and *number_of cabins free* is positive; C people can therefore cross the barrier represented by (2), thus occupying all the cabins, but find themselves blocked by (1). No change in the situation is now possible, because no-one in the pool can get a cabin in which to change and so release a basket. This illustrates the need for a deep analysis of the abstract expression and for a proof that such a situation cannot arise (cf. section 1.2.7), as well as for a check that the program is not in conflict with this analysis.

3.4.3. Comments on the use of semaphores

Semaphores are tools which are particularly well adapted to implementations in which the processes themselves execute the control operations, because they enable limits to be placed on the number of simultaneous operations; clearly, they can be used also to program communication with a control process, such as the control of access to a mail-box. However, they have several disadvantages, as is shown in the above example:

(i) the resulting programs are not easy to read because, in general, the number of operations on the semaphores is large and these are scattered through the process texts;

(ii) it is difficult to construct solutions which can be guaranteed to be correct except by implementing systematically and exactly the abstract expression; and this leads to inefficient solutions.

The methods described in the next section do not have these disadvantages.

3.5. Synchronization mechanisms

The expressions derived in this section assume the existence of a means for imposing mutual exclusion and have equivalents in terms of programming with semaphores; as bases for methods of solution, they have certain advantages which give them a similarity to abstract expressions. The use of the first (section 3.5.1) is quite similar to that of semaphores and corresponds to the method of variables shared directly by the cooperating processes. The second (section 3.5.2) illustrates the case where all the control statements are gathered together in one module, and the third (section 3.5.3) enables control processes to be programmed.

3.5.1. Critical regions

When semaphores are used in a program, nothing prevents a synchronization variable from being used outside a sequence which executes in a mutually exclusive manner; the correct use of shared variables depends entirely on 'good' programming practice that introduces sufficient operations on the semaphores to control access to the variables. The potential difficulty here is avoided by the idea of a **critical region**, introduced by Hoare and Brinch Hansen [Hoare 72; Brinch Hansen 72]; this is defined as a sequence of statements executed in mutual exclusion and according to the use of a variable which has been declared explicity as shared. More precisely, the syntax and semantics of this concept are as follows.

(a) Shared variable declaration:

*var v: **shared** t*

This defines a shared variable *v* of type *t*; here, *t* can be a structured type, enabling several distinct variables to be declared identical as far as sharing is concerned.

(b) Unconditional critical region:

***region** v **do** s*

This states that the sequence of statements *s* accesses the shared variable *v* and is executed in mutual exclusion relative to *v*: i.e. if several processes are attempting simultaneously to execute the regions associated with the same shared variable, only one is allowed to proceed and the others are blocked. One of the waiting processes is re-activated when the active process comes to the end of the sequence *s*.

(c) Conditional critical region:

(i) ***region** v **when** b **do** s*

The critical region *s* is executed only when the Boolean expression *b*, which can include constants or the variable *v*, is true. The execution of this statement by a process *p* is as follows:

— *p* enters the critical region and *b* is evaluated,

— if *b* is true, *p* executes *s* and then leaves the critical region,

— if *b* is false, *p* leaves the critical region and is blocked; it is re-activated when another process leaves the critical region associated with *v*; *p* then restarts by evaluating *b* again.

(ii) ***region** v **do** s **await** b*

The process executes the critical region *s* as in (b) above and then waits until *b* becomes true.

Example

As an illustration of the use of this mechanism, we shall program the procedures *dressing* and *changing* in a form which takes into account the states of the resources *baskets occupied* and *cabins occupied* (cf. sections 1.2.2, 1.2.3).

The two counters, initialized to 0, are combined in the shared variable:

*var resources: **shared record** number_of cabins occupied,*
*number_of baskets occupied: **integer***
end

The condition for permission to change:

number_of cabins occupied $< c$ **and** *number_of baskets occupied* $< b$

can be expressed by a conditional critical region; thus the procedure *changing* is:

start changing
```
region resources
      when number_of cabins occupied < c and
           number_of baskets occupied < b
      do
      begin number_of cabins occupied
                        := number_of cabins occupied + 1 ;
            number_of baskets occupied
                        := number_of baskets occupied + 1 ;
      end ;
```
... *put clothes in basket* ...

finish changing
```
region resources
      do number_of cabins occupied
                        := number_of cabins occupied − 1 ;
```

The procedure *dressing*, controlled by the condition *number_of cabins occupied* $< c$, is programmed similarly:

start dressing
```
region resources
      when number_of cabins occupied < c
      do number_of cabins occupied
                        := number_of cabins occupied + 1 ;
```
... *put on clothes* ...

finish dressing
```
region resources
      do begin number_of cabins occupied
                        := number_of cabins occupied − 1 ;
            number_of baskets occupied
                        := number_of baskets occupied − 1 ;
      end ;
```

The program is a direct representation of the abstract expression; all risk of deadlock is avoided by the use of a single shared variable to hold the two counters, which ensures that these are acquired sequentially.

Comment

The use of critical regions makes it possible for each of a set of cooperating processes to specify the particular operations it wishes to apply to the shared variables; and mutual exclusion is ensured automatically. A critical region can represent a controller equally well, ensuring mutual exclusion among the processes requesting its actions. Static controls can be applied in order to ensure that a shared variable is never used outside a critical region. Furthermore, Gries and Owicki [Owicki 76] have used the critical region concept to develop techniques for proofs relating to the behaviour of parallel systems, by means of which, for example, the impossibility of a program becoming deadlocked can be proved.

The method does, however, suffer from one of the disadvantages noted in the use of semaphores: the critical regions are scattered through the program text.

A close approach to the abstract expression of the problem is made possible by the use of conditional critical regions, because the condition for allowing an operation to be executed can be expressed in the language whilst the blocking and resumption of processes occur implicitly. This, however, has the disadvantage that too frequent, and often unnecessary, evaluations of conditions have to be made because blocked processes can be re-activated before the conditions which blocked them have changed. Sintzoff and Van Lamsweerde [Sintzoff 75] have suggested an extension to the method which limits the number of conditions to be recalculated at each synchronization event. We shall now give a different method, due to Schmid [Schmid 76], which ensures that a process is re-activated only if it can continue.

Similar optimization methods can be used with tools other than critical regions; the essence is the use of selective re-activations so as to speed up the execution of statements of the form **wait** condition (see, for example [La Palme 80]).

AUTOMATIC OPTIMIZATION

The improvement sought is a reduction in the number of evaluations of blocking conditions; for this, we look for the **static** relations among the different critical regions, i.e. the relations which do not change during execution. These are the program invariants which can therefore be determined by a compiler for example, before execution.

For critical regions in the form:

$$R_i : \textbf{\textit{region}} \; v \; \textbf{\textit{when}} \; C_i \; \textbf{\textit{do}} \; Op_i \; ;$$

the relations we seek are:

(a) the 'enabling' relation: two critical regions R_i and R_j do not satisfy such a relation if the operation Op_i can never cause the condition C_j to become true;

(b) the 'disabling' relation: two critical regions R_i and R_j do not satisfy such a relation if the operation Op_i can never cause the condition C_j to become false.

Theorems by means of which such relations can be derived automatically are given in [Schmid 76].

For the swimming-pool example above, the relations between the critical regions associated with the shared variable *resources* are:

enabling: *(finish changing, start changing),*
                            (finish changing, start dressing),
                            (finish dressing, start changing),
                            (finish dressing, start dressing).

disabling: *(start changing, start dressing),*
                            (start changing, start changing),
                            (start dressing, start changing),
                            (start dressing, start dressing).

The second phase of the optimization process involves the insertion of operations for testing, activating or blocking processes which are in one or other of these relations to one another, at appropriate points in the program texts. Handling of the queues of waiting processes is programmed explicitly. For example, since *finish changing* is an enabling relation with *start changing* and also with *start dressing*, we may include in *finish changing* the tests and activations corresponding to the other two. An automatic system would produce a program equivalent in operation to:

region *resources*
    do begin
       number_of cabins occupied := *number_of cabins occupied* − 1 ;
       if *number_of cabins occupied* < *c* **and** $\left.\begin{array}{l}\end{array}\right\}$ *test for*
          number_of baskets occupied < *b*   *start changing*
          then *unblock-one (waiting to change)* ;

       if *number_of cabins occupied* < *c* $\left.\begin{array}{l}\end{array}\right\}$ *test for*
          then *unblock-one (waiting to dress)* ; *start dressing*

    end

Here, a program which has been activated no longer has to check its condition; and in a multi-programmed system there are no unnecessary context switches.

3.5.2. Monitors

A monitor [Brinch Hansen 73; Hoare 74] is a syntactic entity (a module) which groups the synchronization variables and shared resources with the procedures which act on them. This avoids the disadvantage of the operations which access the shared variables being scattered through the process code. The variables declared in the monitor are, by definition, accessible only to the monitor procedures, some of which will be purely internal to the monitor, whilst others may be called from outside the monitor; the latter form the **entry points** to the monitor.

Two types of synchronization are defined in a monitor:

(i) mutual exclusion between the monitor procedures, implemented implicitly. This is analogous to the mutual exclusion between criticial regions associated with the same variable;

(ii) explicit definition of synchronization variables, declared as *condition* variables, to which the operators *wait, signal* and *empty* can be applied. A process which executes *wait* is suspended and held in the queue associated implicitly with a condition until that condition is satisfied. *Empty* checks if a queue is empty. *Signal* c re-activates *one* process (assuming there is at least one) which is waiting on condition c and, to ensure mutual exclusion, the process which has executed the *signal* operation is itself suspended and remains so as long as there are active processes in the monitor. As each process leaves the monitor, either by coming to the end of a procedure or by performing a *wait* operation, the monitor checks that there are no processes halted by a *signal* operation before admitting another process waiting at an entry point; if there are such processes, one is re-activated.

Example — the swimming-pool again

We use a monitor for the shared variables *number_of cabins occupied* and *number_of baskets occupied*, and for the access procedures which implement the operations *start changing, finish changing, start dressing, finish dressing*. We need two **condition** variables to express waiting on a condition for changing or dressing, for which we have chosen *basket free* and *cabin free*. The program is as follows:

```
swimming pool: monitor ;
    number_of baskets occupied, number_of cabins occupied: integer ;
    basket free, cabin free: condition ;
    procedure start changing ;
        begin
            if number_of baskets occupied = b then wait basket free ;
                number_of baskets occupied := number_of baskets occupied + 1 ;
            if number_of cabins occupied = c then wait cabin free ;
                number_of cabins occupied := number_of cabins occupied + 1 ;
        end ;
    procedure finish changing ;
        begin
                number_of cabins occupied := number_of cabins occupied − 1 ;
                signal cabin free
        end ;
    procedure start dressing ;
        begin
            if number_of cabins occupied = c then wait cabin free ;
                number_of cabins occupied := number_of cabins occupied + 1 ;
        end ;
    procedure finish dressing ;
        begin
```

number_of baskets occupied := *number_of baskets occupied* − *1* ;
number_of cabins occupied := *number_of cabins occupied* − *1* ;
signal *basket free*
signal *cabin free*
end ;
begin
number_of baskets occupied := *0* ; *number_of cabins occupied* := *0* ;
end ;

The order in which **signal** operations and the operations which change the values of the variables are executed is of great importance: before signalling that a condition holds, it is essential to ensure that the states of the variables are consistent with that condition. In the above, for example, the **signal** operations must not be placed at the head of the procedure *finish dressing*. As in the case of a program using semaphores, deadlocks can result from certain orderings of the *wait* operations (see section 3.4.2). It would have been possible, in this example, to have used a single condition for *cabin free* **and** *basket free* (to be used for *start changing*) and one for *cabin free* (to be used for *start dressing*), but then the **signal** operations in *finish dressing* would have been more complex. Finally, the order in which the **signal** operations are given can determine the relative priorities of the various processes.

Comments

As far as efficiency is concerned, all the procedures in a monitor are mutually exclusive and this is not always necessary; in particular, when certain procedures require that several variables are gathered together in the same monitor, those procedures which use only a subset of these variables do not need to be in a state of mutual exclusion with respect to all the others. Furthermore, there is often a tendency to use the modular structure of a monitor to group together all the synchronization actions which one needs, together with the control statements themselves; this results in all these actions being mutually exclusive, even though this may not be necessary.

One of the main disadvantages of the monitor idea lies in the use of the **signal** primitive. As we have seen in the above example, the statements associated with this can be located anywhere in the body of a procedure, and an ill-chosen order can result in an erroneous policy for freeing halted processes. Proof techniques for ensuring proper use of **wait** and **signal** have been developed by Howard [Howard 76]. Variants of the idea have been proposed, aimed at avoiding this difficulty without unduly complicating the handling of the processes which perform the **signal** operations; we deal with these in the following paragraph.

KESSEL'S CONDITIONS

The **condition** operation developed by Kessel [Kessel 77] enables us to use conditional waits with automatic re-activation. In a monitor, Boolean expressions can be defined under the name *condition* and associated with identifiers; when a *wait* operator acts on such a condition name, the expression is evaluated and the process is suspended if the result is false. Conditions are re-evaluated when any process leaves the monitor or becomes blocked, and, if one is true, one of the suspended processes is re-activated. This method is similar to that of the re-evaluation of conditions at the end of critical regions (section 3.5.1): there are no explicit *signal* primitives. We can then program the swimming-pool problem as follows:

```
swimming-pool: monitor
        number_of baskets occupied, number_of cabins occupied: integer ;
        cabin free: condition number_of cabins occupied < c ;
        cabin and basket free: condition number_of baskets
                        occupied < b and number_of cabins occupied < c ;
    procedure start changing ;
        begin wait cabin and basket free ;
            number_of baskets occupied := number_of baskets occupied + 1 ;
            number_of cabins occupied := number_of cabins occupied + 1 ;
        end ;
    procedure finish changing ;
        number_of cabins occupied := number_of cabins occupied − 1 ;
    procedure start dressing ;
        begin wait cabin free ;
            number_of cabins occupied := number_of cabins occupied + 1 ;
        end ;
    procedure finish dressing ;
        begin number_of cabins occupied := number_of cabins occupied − 1 ;
            number_of baskets occupied := number_of baskets occupied − 1 ;
        end ;
    begin
        number_of cabins occupied := 0 ; number_of baskets occupied := 0 ;
    end ;
```

This form is more easily readable, and the same means for optimization can be used as for critical regions in order to improve performance.

3.5.3. Writing a control interpreter in Ada[1]

The preceding methods are all concerned specifically with synchronization; in contrast, we now describe a way of programming an interpreter for control expressions. Any programming language can be used for this purpose provided that it enables communication between processes to be expressed; we have chosen the recent language, Ada [ASRM 83], which includes the con-

---

[1] Ada is a registered trademark of the United States Government, Ada Joint Program Office.

cept of parallel processes. Tools for communication and synchronization have therefore been provided in the language, some being very well adapted to the expression of control functions. The book by Le Verrand [Le Verrand 85] on the evaluation of Ada can be consulted for details of the language.

DEFINITIONS

(a) Communication with blocking

The statement *accept x(p) do s end* causes a process to wait until a call of type x, possibly with parameters p, is received from another process, and to execute a sequence s when the call is received. The call is blocking, i.e. the calling process cannot resume until the execution of s has been completed. Since a process can execute only one *accept* statement at a time, if there are several in the same process this ensures that execution is mutually exclusive; and this corresponds to the manner in which communication between the controller and the cooperating processes is required to be conducted (see section 3.3.1). x is declared in the controller as an *entry point*, and in the calling process a sync-point takes the form of a call statement.

(b) Conditional wait

The handling of a call can be made conditional by means of the statement *when condition ⇒ accept x do s end*. This provides a natural way in which conditions governing the execution of processes associated with a sync-point can be programmed.

(c) Multiple wait

A non-deterministic control structure of the form *select s1 or s2 or ... end* expresses the fact that a choice may be made between a number of sequences. If these are *accept* statements, it makes it possible to cause the controller to wait for messages of different types.

(d) Uncontrolled calls to procedures

A call to an entry point is not the only form of communication between processes in Ada. A process can call and can execute, **within its own scope**, a public procedure which has been declared in a **package** (a module of program). Several processes can therefore access the same objects indirectly through the medium of a package. There is no control on a call of this type and several procedure evaluations can take place in parallel.

COMMENTS

A treatment of the swimming-pool problem in Ada has been given in section 1.2.3. This shows that the programming of the controller follows directly from the abstract expression for the problem by use of the synchronization methods provided in the language, i.e. blocking calls, conditional waits and mutual exclusion between entry points. The efficiency of the treatment, however, depends on the way in which the wait conditions (the conditional expressions following *when*) are evaluated, and can be low; the difficulty, here, is similar to that concerning the re-evaluation of conditions in critical regions.

In contrast, the existence of public procedures which are not executed by the controller makes it possible to use a single entity (the Ada **package**) in which to define variables, including resources, procedures to handle them, and any related control operations, and to do so without imposing any mutual exclusion on those procedures. If monitors (see section 3.5.3) are used, this grouping cannot be made without some constraints being imposed on the execution.

3.6. Evaluation of the preceding methods

The methods we have described in section 3.5, and all those which are similar to them, are equivalent to the extent that they enable all the standard synchronization problems to be programmed, and they can all be expressed in terms of semaphores, considered as the basic tool. They differ in the ease of expression of the problem which they make possible: implementation starting from the abstract expression is more or less direct, according to the method used. Their use is illustrated in section 3.7, where the stages in the programming of one problem, that of 'readers/writers', are given for each of the different methods. It is difficult to make any absolute classification of the methods with respect to ease of expression, because the facilities they offer are individually adapted to the different types of problem. They can, however, be compared from the points of view of readability, ease of changing the control strategy, security and performance; we now consider these in turn.

3.6.1. Readability and ease of modification

As far as readability is concerned, a study of programs for cooperating processes shows that there are advantages in the use of monitors or interpreters: the control statements do not appear in the process texts, whereas they do in the case of critical regions or semaphores. For the same reason, modifications are easier to make when these methods are used, because they will now be more localized.

However, this particular disadvantage of critical regions vanishes if a compiler or macrogenerator is available which can correctly insert the necessary synchronization instructions automatically. Furthermore, with monitors and interpreters the problems of expression carry through to the programming of the controller, and if tools well adapted for communication (such as those of

Ada) are not available, the interpreter can be very complex. We have shown that with monitors it can be difficult to program the re-activation of processes; more precisely, it can be difficult to decide which processes to re-activate when the state variables have been changed. Viewed from this angle, the readability and ease of modification associated with monitors are less evident; the use of automatic tools, which remove the need for programming the re-activation of halted processes explicitly, brings about a significant improvement.

3.6.2. Security

Except in the case of direct use of semaphores, access to those state variables which are needed for synchronization is controlled and occurs in a mutually exclusive manner in the critical regions, the monitor procedures or the controllers. Normally, this ensures consistency.

A point not discussed so far is the reliability of these methods, meaning their security in case of system failures. Although there are important problems here, the question has been little studied: what happens, for example, if a process fails while it is executing a critical region in a mutually exclusive manner? No fault-tolerant mechanisms have been built into the synchronization tools apart from those that we have described. In distributed systems, for which one of the fundamental requirements is resistance to failures, fault-tolerant mechanisms form an explicit part of the means for achieving synchronization (see chapter 4).

3.6.3. Performance

An estimate of the performance of each of these methods can be obtained either from the use of mutual exclusion or from the frequency of context switches, the latter being related to the number of evaluations required of the synchronization conditions.

For the first, the greatest efficiency results from the use of semaphores or critical regions because tools of this type enable mutual exclusion to be programmed at the simplest level, i.e. at the level of the variables; they reduce to a minimum the amount of exclusion necessary to ensure coherence among the operations. Their advantage over monitors is even greater when the monitors are used to program both the controller and the procedures that are to be controlled, such as the procedures for the use of resources.

If we base our estimate on frequency of context switches, we have to consider that processes are suspended until the relevant conditions are true, and their re-activation is brought about in various ways which can be quite costly:

— after every change in the values of the state variables, the processes are freed and they themselves decide whether or not they can continue by re-evaluating the conditions which caused them to be blocked. Use of this method, as with critical regions, imposes penalties because it results in changes in the processes' states which serve no useful purpose;

— after every change in the values of the state variables, all the conditions are re-evaluated and only one process for which the condition is true is re-activated: this is the case with Kessel's monitors. The cost incurred here is that of the re-evaluations, but the only processes freed are those which are known to be able to continue;

— only those conditions which may have changed are re-evaluated, and one process is freed if this is possible. This is the case when *signal* primitives are used explicitly with monitors.

This categorization could clearly be affected by the existence of automatic means for optimizing the re-evaluation of conditions and the freeing of processes, as, for example, in the case of critical regions.

This last comment applies in fact to all the points we have studied, because the use of automatic tools can compensate for differences between the methods. This leads to the possibility of envisaging a completely automatic procedure for translating the abstract expression into a program; whilst this has not yet been achieved, it could be approached in the following way:

(a) analyse the synchronization problem at the level of the abstract expression,

(b) use a programming tool of as high a level as possible for an implementation of this expression,

(c) finally, by means of a compiler, macrogenerator or otherwise, introduce improvements to compensate for the likely inefficiencies of the high level language.

3.7. Implementation of the abstract expression of the 'reader/writer' problem, for a centralized system

We show how different forms of the abstract expression for solving problems of the 'reader/writer' type [Courtois 71] can be obtained, using the methods of chapter 2, and then give implementations for a centralized system using the tools described in chapter 3.

3.7.1. The reader/writer problem without explicitly defined priorities

Consider a set of processes which access a common file, either simply to consult it (readers) or to modify it (writers). Reading operations can take place simultaneously and in parallel, but simultaneous modifications are prohibited and reading is not allowed during a modification operation (to ensure the consistency of the file and the information read from it).

(a) The expression for the synchronization conditions in terms of control modules [Robert 77] is as follows.

readwrite: **control module**
 begin
  condition *(read): # exec (write) = 0 ;*
  condition *(write): # exec (read) + # exec (write) = 0 ;*
 end

(b) In terms of synchronization controllers [Pulou 78] the expression is:

sync-points: *startread, finishread, startwrite, finishwrite*
 integer variables *numberwrite = 0, numberread = 0*
startread ⟷ **condition** *numberwrite = 0 ;*
       transformation *numberread := numberread + 1 ;*
finishread ⟷ **condition** *true ;*
       transformation *numberread := numberread − 1 ;*
startwrite ⟷ **condition** *numberwrite = 0* **and** *numberread = 0 ;*
       transformation *numberwrite := numberwrite + 1 ;*
finishwrite ⟷ **condition** *true ;*
       transformation *numberwrite := numberwrite − 1 ;*

(c) To express the conditions in terms of synchronization words [Roucairol 78] we first define two alphabets $\Sigma_r = \{r\}$ and $\Sigma_w = \{w\}$, and two synchronization words M_r and M_w. A letter r is placed in M_r when a read operation is taking place and a letter w in M_w when writing. λ denotes the empty word.

Initialization: $M_r \leftarrow \lambda$; $M_w \leftarrow \lambda$

reader   **writer**
TEST (M_w:λ) APPEND (M_r:r)   *TEST (M_w:λ, M_r:λ) APPEND (M_w:w)*
  read   *write*
DELETE (M_r:r)   *DELETE (M_w:w)*

(d) Finally, in terms of path expressions [Campbell 74], the conditions are simply:

 path *{R}, W* **end**

Note: All the above expressions could give rise to a starvation of writers, brought about by a coalition among the readers; furthermore, since no priority is specified, the writers could be favoured, resulting in a temporary starvation of readers.

3.7.2. Implementation for a centralized system

(a) SEMAPHORES

A semaphore *W* ensures exclusive access for a writer; it is initialized to 1, must be acquired using the function *P* before each *write* operation, and is released at the end of that operation; it can also be modified by the first reader, to test if reading is allowed, and by the last, to release access. A second semaphore R ensures that the operations of counting the number of readers are atomic; the integer variable nr is defined for this purpose.

reader	**writer**
P(R)	*P(W)*
nr := nr + 1 ;	*write*
if *nr = 1* **then** *P(W)* **endif**	*V(W)*
V(R)	
read	
P(R)	
nr := nr − 1 ;	
if *nr = 0* **then** *V(W)* **endif**	
V(R)	

This form gives the readers priority over the writers, with the possibility of a famine of the latter.

(b) CRITICAL REGIONS

var v: **shared record** *nr, nw:* **integer end**
    (number of readers and writers, respectively)

reader:	**writer:**
region *v* **when**	**region** *v* **when** *nr = 0* **and**
nw = 0 **do** *nr := nr + 1 ;*	*nw = 0* **do** *nw := 1 ;*
read	*write*
region *v* **do** *nr := nr − 1 ;*	**region** *v* **do** *nw := 0 ;*

(c) MONITORS: TWO SOLUTIONS

(1) A direct translation of the abstract expression, here in terms of control modules, gives the following monitor; nr is the number of readers and nw the number of writers.

file access: **monitor** *;*
  nr, nw: **integer** *;*
  qread, qwrite: **condition** *;*
  procedure *start read ;*
    begin
      if not *(nw ≤ 0)* **then wait** *qread ;*
      nr := nr + 1 ;
    end *;*
  procedure *finish read ;*
    begin
      nr := nr − 1 ;
      while *(nw ≤ 0)* **and** *(nr ≤ 0)* **and not empty** *qwrite*
        do signal *qwrite ;*
    end *;*

```
procedure start write ;
   begin
      if not ((nw ≤ 0) and (nr ≤ 0)) then wait qwrite ;
      nw := nw + 1 ;
   end ;
procedure finish write ;
   begin
      nw := nw − 1 ;
      while (nw ≤ 0) and (nr ≤ 0) and not empty qwrite
            do signal qwrite ;
      while (nw ≤ 0) and not empty qread do signal qread ;
   end ;
begin
   nr := 0 ; nw := 0 ;
end monitor ;
```

(2) The previous monitor can be simplified by taking into account the following:

(a) if one reader is allowed to proceed, so can all those that are waiting,

(b) at most, one writer can be executing at any one time,

(c) a *signal* on an empty queue has no effect.

This leads to the following program:

```
file access: monitor ;
       nr, nw: integer ;
       qread, qwrite: condition ;
procedure start read ;
   begin
      if nw ≠ 0 then wait qread ;
      nr := nr + 1 ;
      signal qread ;
   end ;
procedure finish read ;
   begin
      nr := nr − 1 ;
      if nr = 0 then signal qwrite ;
   end ;
procedure start write ;
   begin
      if nw ≠ 0 or nr > 0 then wait qwrite ;
      nw := 1 ;
   end ;
procedure finish write ;
   begin
      nw := 0 ;
```

> **if not empty** qwrite **then signal** qwrite **else signal** qread ;
> **end** ;
begin
    nr := 0 ; nw := 0 ;
end monitor ;

Note: Any particular implementation can introduce priorities which are not specified in the abstract expression.

3.7.3. Expressing priority given to the writer

The situation is now modified so that when a writer arrives it is served as quickly as possible. Using control modules, the modified expression differs only in the condition for allowing reading, as follows:

condition (read): # wait (write) = 0 **and** # exec (write) = 0 ;

For the synchronization word method, a word M_x can be used to record the number of attempts made to write; we then have:

Initializations: $M_r \leftarrow \lambda$; $M_w \leftarrow \lambda$; $M_x \leftarrow \lambda$;

reader	**writer**
TEST $(M_x{:}\lambda)$ APPEND $(M_r{:}r)$	APPEND $(M_x{:}w)$
read	TEST $(M_w{:}\lambda, M_r{:}\lambda)$ APPEND $(M_w{:}w)$
DELETE $(M_r{:}r)$	write
	DELETE $(M_w{:}w, M_x{:}w)$

3.7.4. An implementation with writer priority

The following uses critical regions, with the notations:

waitwrite: number of writers waiting
nr: number of readers active
nw: number of writers active

var v: **shared record** waitwrite, nr, nw: **integer end**
        initialized to 0

reader:

region v
  when waitwrite ≤ 0 **and** nw ≤ 0
    do nr := nr + 1 ;
  read
region v **do** nr := nr − 1 ;

writer:

region v **do** waitwrite := waitwrite + 1;
region v **when** nr ≤ 0 **and** nw ≤ 0
  do
    begin
      nw := nw + 1 ;
      waitwrite := waitwrite − 1 ;
    end ;
  write
region v **do** nw := nw − 1 ;

3.7.5. Avoiding reader starvation

Here, we take up Hoare's proposals again, described in section 2.3.2, of which two expressions were given in sections 2.3.3 and 2.3.4. We now consider their implementation using monitors.

We first make a direct translation of the abstract expression, using queues A, R, W of section 2.3.3 and four counters:

waitw: number waiting to write, in W
execw: number in the course of writing
waitrp: number waiting to read, with priority, in R
execr: number in the course of reading

```
file: monitor
        begin waitw, execw, waitrp, execr: integer := 0 ;
            A, R, W: condition ;
        procedure start read ;
            begin
                if waitw ≠ 0 and execw ≠ 1
                    then begin A.wait ; A.signal end ;
                if execw ≠ 0 then
                    begin waitrp +:= 1 ;
                          R.wait ;
                          waitrp −:= 1 ;
                          R.signal ;   co to release all readers co
                    end ;
                        execr +:= 1 ;
            end ;
        procedure finish read ;
            begin execr −:= 1 ;
                if execr = 0 and waitrp = 0 then W.signal ;
            end ;
        procedure start write ;
            begin
                if execr ≠ 0 or execw ≠ 0 or waitrp ≠ 0 then
                    begin waitw +:= 1 ;
                          W.wait ;
                          waitw −:= 1 ;
                    end ;
            execw +:= 1 ; A.signal ;
            end ;
        procedure finish write ;
            begin execw −:= 1 ;
                if waitrp ≠ 0 then R.signal
                                else W.signal ;
            end ;
```

We can now simplify this monitor. If there is a writer waiting, the effect of queue A is to block those readers which arrive in the interval between a writer leaving the file (at time t), after completing its writing operation, and the last of the readers which have been released at time t leaving queue R. When the properties of monitors are taken into account, it is seen that these readers are automatically blocked outside the monitor; the queue A can therefore be dispensed with, and the result of doing so is a monitor similar to that given in chapter 3.

Chapter 4

Distributed implementation

4.1. Introduction

The design and construction of distributed computer systems is a relatively new field of endeavour and it is not yet possible to identify methods and tools which have universal acceptance. An attempt to give a unified treatment of distributed synchronization problems would therefore be premature, so our aim in this chapter is simply to point to the difficulties of distributing control and to demonstrate some basic methods which have been proposed as a means of attacking these difficulties. The examples given in the last part of the chapter illustrate the use of these methods in control algorithms adapted to the needs of particular situations.

4.1.1. Distributed architecture and control

We define here a simple form of distributed architecture and lay down conditions which apply to all the mechanisms described later.

A distributed architecture is a system of connected sites in which each site has its own private memory; there is no common memory. We assume:

(i) Every site can communicate directly with every other — i.e. the system forms a logical network.

(ii) Transmission is error-free.

(iii) For transmission between any pair of sites i and j, the order in which i sends messages to j is the same as the order in which j receives the messages. In particular, there is no loss of messages.

(iv) Any breakdown of a site (or, equivalently, its physical isolation from the rest of the system) is detected and signalled to all sites which attempt to communicate with it.

Our problem is how to introduce into such an architecture the abstract machinery which describes the synchronization constraints. We can envisage solutions of the same types as those proposed for a centralized system in chapter 3 (section 3.3), i.e.:

(a) Centralized control: this is a trivial solution, consisting in gathering together on a single site all the variables and statements needed for the synchronization. Execution is brought about by a single process, the **master controller**, to which all the processes residing in the different sites send messages. The situation then becomes exactly that of a centralized system, with no parallelism (inside the master controller) and with reliability dependent on a privileged site, and offers the same possibilities for programming.

(b) Distributed control: distributing the control over the different sites leads to the need to consider N **control processes,** one at each site. Each local controller handles the processes located on its site and all cooperate via the communication system to implement the abstract expressions. This type of organization, which we have called **distributed control,** gives rise to difficulties which we shall study in this chapter; they are illustrated by the simple example below.

4.1.2. Introductory example

OBSERVING THE EVENTS

Consider the producer/consumer problem in which now, in order to avoid overflow in the buffers, the number of items produced is restricted to no more than N greater than the number consumed. The only constraints on the relative orders in which productions and consumptions can be made are those given in Fig. 1, where $a \rightarrow b$ means that event a precedes event b, and P_i, C_i denote the ith production and consumption respectively.

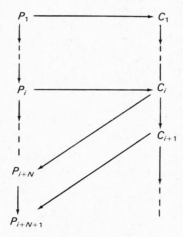

Fig. 1. *Producer/consumer problem: precedence constraints.*

As in chapter 2, we introduce the instantaneous events

start (x) and *finish (x)*

to represent the start and end respectively of action x; then if $\#\,c$ represents the number of events of class c, the synchronization condition can be expressed by the two following invariants:

$$\# \; start \; (cons) \leq \# \; finish \; (prod) \tag{1}$$
$$\# \; start \; (prod) - \# \; finish \; (cons) \leq N \tag{2}$$

Consider, initially, the implementation shown in Fig. 2.

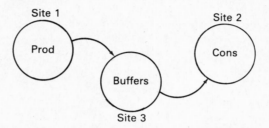

Fig. 2. *Producer/consumer problem on a distributed architecture.*

The following four counters are observable quantities on the given sites:

$\# \; start \; (prod)$: *site 1*
$\# \; finish \; (prod)$: *site 3*
$\# \; start \; (cons)$: *site 2*
$\# \; finish \; (cons)$: *site 3*

To allow production to occur, the condition

$$\# \; start \; (prod) - \# \; finish \; (cons) < N \tag{3}$$

must hold, which requires a knowledge of the value of $\#\ finish\ (cons)$ as observed on site 3. Whether site 1 requests this value periodically from site 3, or the latter advises site 1 whenever the value changes, the time taken for transmission between the two sites means that there is a delay before site 1 is informed of the value of $\#\ finish\ (cons)$. It is as if site 1 had a delayed image $\#\ \overline{finish}\ (cons)$ of $\#\ finish\ (cons)$, with

$$\#\ \overline{finish}\ (cons) \leq \#\ finish\ (cons)$$

since these values increase monotonically with time.

Thus, if the producer checks before each production that the condition

$$\#\ start\ (prod) - \#\ \overline{finish}\ (cons) < N$$

holds, then condition (3) is satisfied and invariant (2) is not contradicted. Similarly, the consumer at site 2, with a corresponding image $\#\ \overline{finish}\ (prod)$ such that

$$\#\ \overline{finish}\ (prod) \leq \#\ finish\ (prod)$$

must, before consuming, check that

$$\#\ start\ (cons) < \#\ \overline{finish}\ (prod)$$

Thus it can happen, for example (see Fig. 3), that:

(a) from the point of view of the producer, three productions have been started before it is aware of any consumption having been finished; for the producer, the sequence of events is

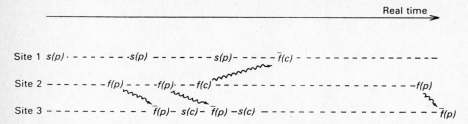

Fig. 3. *Timings of events: s(p) start production, f(p) finish production, etc. Transmission times, indicated by* ∿∿∿ *, can be of any magnitude.*

$$s(p) \quad s(p) \quad s(p) \quad \overline{f}(c) \quad \dots$$

(b) from the point of view of the consumer, the sequence of events is

$$\overline{f}(p) \quad s(c) \quad \overline{f}(p) \quad s(c) \quad \overline{f}(p) \quad \dots$$

(c) on site 3, the sequence is seen as

$$f(p) \quad f(p) \quad f(c) \quad f(p) \quad \dots$$

(d) if the true situation could be observed, it would be seen to be

$$s(p) \quad f(p) \quad s(p) \quad f(p) \quad s(c) \quad f(c) \quad s(p) \quad s(c) \quad f(p)$$

The time traces recorded at each site are called **partial traces** and the real trace, given in (d), is called the **theoretical trace**. This trace must be a statement in a language L which forms the abstract expression for the synchronization, on which local constraints of sufficient rigour have been imposed to ensure that the legality of the set of partial traces implies the legality of the theoretical trace.

Example

Let the constraint imposed at site 2 be:

$$\overline{f_i\,(p)} \rightarrow s_i\,(c)$$

Since the transmission time for a message is non-zero, it is always true that:

$$f_i\,(p) \rightarrow \overline{f_i\,(p)}$$

from which it follows that:

$$f_i\,(p) \rightarrow s_i\,(c)$$

which is the property required for the analysis of the problem.

The treatment of the previous example becomes simpler when the buffer is located on either site 1 or site 2. This is represented in Fig. 4 and the program in Ada [ASRM 83] is as follows, taking the case of the buffer on site 2.

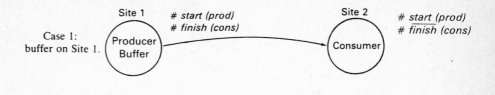

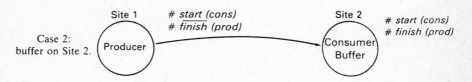

Fig. 4. *Producer/consumer problem, two sites only.*

Site 1

The variables defined at this site are:

> *STRTPROD* and *FINCONS':* both initialized to 0
> where *FINCONS'* represents # *finish (cons)*
>   *V* is a working variable

The process at this site is:

> **task** *PRODUCER ;*
> **task** *SERVERP* **is**
>   **entry** *PRODUCE*
> **end** *SERVERP ;*
> **task** *RECEIVERSITE1* **is**
>   **entry** *FINCONSUME*
> **end** *RECEIVERSITE1 ;*

The bodies of these tasks are:

> **task body** *PRODUCER* **is**
>   **begin**
>   **loop**
>   *... elaboration of a value V ...*
>   *SERVERP.PRODUCE ;*   -- awaiting permission to produce
>   *RECEIVERSITE2.FILL(V) ;* -- sends the value of *V* to site 2
>   **end loop**
>   **end** *PRODUCER ;*

```
task body SERVERP is
    begin
        loop
            when STRTPROD − FINCONS' < N ⇒ accept PRODUCE ;
                STRTPROD := STRTPROD + 1 ;
        end loop ;
    end SERVERP ;

task body RECEIVERSITE1 is
    begin
        loop
            accept FINCONSUME ;                    -- message from site 2
                FINCONS' := FINCONS' + 1 ;
        end loop ;
    end RECEIVERSITE1 ;
```

Site 2

The variables here are:

BUFFER, IPROD and ICONS : local processing
STRTCONS and FINPROD   : both initialized to 0
S is a working variable

The process at this site is:

```
task CONSUMER ;
task SERVERC is
    entry STRTCONSUME
end SERVERC ;
task RECEIVERSITE2 is
    entry FILL
end RECEIVERSITE2 ;

task body RECEIVERSITE2 is
    begin
        loop
            accept FILL (V: in VALUE) ;            -- value from site 1
            BUFFER [IPROD] := V ;
            IPROD := IPROD + 1 mod N ;
            FINPROD := FINPROD + 1
        end loop
    end RECEIVERSITE2 ;

task body SERVERC is
    begin
        loop
            when STRTCONS < FINPROD ⇒ accept STRTCONSUME ;
            STRTCONS := STRTCONS + 1
```

```
        end loop
    end SERVERC ;

task body CONSUMER is
    begin
        loop
            SERVERC.STRTCONSUME ;
            S := BUFFER [ICONS] ;
            ICONS := ICONS + 1 mod N ;
            RECEIVERSITE1 FINCONSUME ;
                                    -- signals end of consumption for site 1
            ... operations on S ...
        end loop
    end CONSUMER ;
```

Note: No purpose would be served by processing the variables *FINCONS*, *FINPROD'*, *STRTPROD'* and *STRTCONS'*, therefore this has not been programmed.

The programs for the two sites are independent apart from the operations of sending and receiving messages. The procedures at either site handle only the variables local to that site and no global mutual exclusion is imposed. The example illustrates the ease with which we can get away from the idea of a uniquely-represented variable which is handled in a mutually exclusive manner[1]: we simply duplicate the variable and arrange matters so that there is a loose but controlled consistency between the two copies. A more formal account of the techniques for dealing with the resulting uncertainties is given in section 4.5.

ORDERING THE EVENTS

Let us now extend the situation exemplified above to a number of producers sharing the N buffers located at the consumer's site, adding a further rule to ensure **consistency** and **equitability** in the operations of the producers: each producer must put the information it produces in a buffer in finite time and the contents of the buffer must not be overwritten by another producer before they have been used. The invariants are as before, the counters # *start (prod)* and # *finish (prod)* now giving the totals of the productions started and finished, respectively, by all the producers taken together.

The condition for allowing production to take place

$$\# \ start \ (prod) - \# \ finish \ (cons) < N$$

is tested, in principle, for each producer in turn, thus ensuring that a free buffer can be used by only one producer at a time.

As in the previous case, that of a single producer with buffers at the consumer's site, the values of # *start (cons)* and # *finish (prod)* are known

---

[1] This also applies in a centralized system, but the advantage then is less (cf. section 3.2.2).

exactly at the consumer's site; these can therefore be represented by the variables *STRTCONS* and *FINPROD*, respectively, which are processed locally by the consumer. The counters *# start (prod)* and *# finish (cons)* are used by all the producers and by the consumer; one way to manage these would be to cause a message carrying their values — which, because of delays, could only be approximations to the true values — to circulate around all the processes. The method is as follows:

(a) The processes (productions and consumption) are organized to form a **virtual communication ring** as in Fig. 5; the messages pass from one to the next, in a fixed direction.

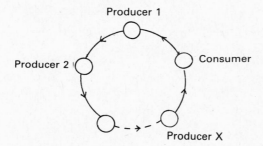

Fig. 5. *'Virtual ring' of producers and consumer.*

(b) A special *control message* circulates around the ring, carrying two items of information, *STRTPROD* and *FINCONS'*, giving the values of the two counters.

(c) A producer wishing to start its next production waits until it receives the control message before testing the condition for permission

$$STRTPROD - FINCONS' < N$$

— If this is true, the producer increases the value of *STRTPROD* by 1 and sends this to its successor on the ring; it can then send its data message to the consumer. If the result is false, the producer merely transmits the control message and waits for its next passage.

(d) When the consumer receives the control message, it adds to *FINCONS'* the number of consumption operations completed since the last receipt of this message.

This method ensures that the first set of abstract synchronization conditions is satisfied, for the following reasons:

— Because there is only a single control message, the condition for permission to produce is evaluated for only one producer at a time, as is the incrementation of *STRTPROD*.

— *FINCONS'* is a delayed image of *# finish(cons)* and we have already shown that its use in place of *# finish(cons)* does not contravene the invariants of the problem.

The method does not, however, guarantee equitability among the producers; in fact, those which are nearest to the consumer on the ring have priority because they are the first to test the condition for production after *FINCONS'* has been modified, and if there are fewer free buffers than there are requests for production then the producers at the 'end' of the ring are starved of service. To remedy this, an order must be established among the production requests, and to do this in a distributed system requires there to be a **protocol** for bringing about cooperation among the processes. We shall show in section 4.4 that this is needed not only to deal with problems of equitability and priority but also to ensure that there are identical copies of the same item of information at the different sites. The following section gives two means for providing this basic tool in distributed implementations.

4.2. Scheduling in distributed systems

We are seeking to establish a **strict total ordering** among the events; this must encompass two concepts of temporal order:

(i) Of any two events in the same process, one must precede the other in time (this is made necessary by the structure of the process).

(ii) The event of sending a message by a process must precede that of its receipt by another.

The synchronization process ensures that, on each site, an order of events is constructed which is compatible with the above temporal relations: for example, for Fig. 6 the order is:

$$a_1\ b_1\ a_2\ b_2\ b_3\ c_1\ a_3\ ...$$

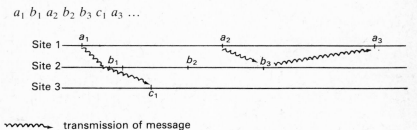

transmission of message

Fig. 6. *Order of events in a distributed system.*

This ordering is possibly different from the true temporal relationships that an external observer would see on the set of three sites.

There are two principal methods for arriving at such an ordering.

(a) Circulation of a message around a virtual ring

A special message circulates around all the processes concerned, organized in a virtual ring as described in section 4.1.2. This carries a value giving the number of the current event in the sequence. To time-stamp an event, a process must await the arrival of this message, extract the order number (time of the event), and then increment the value contained in the message.

This simple method has the disadvantage that if the message is lost, the system is brought to a halt; in section 4.7 we shall consider ways to overcome this.

(b) Use of 'logical clocks'

We should like to time-stamp each event by means of a single clock, capable of being read instantaneously. To achieve this in a distributed system we arrange for each site to have a copy of a hypothetical clock or stamp, and we ensure the consistency of these copies as follows.

Initially, all the copies are set to zero. Whenever a site S_i reads the value of its clock C_i, it performs the following:

— remove the current value of C_i;

— increase C_i by 1;

— send a message to all other sites so that they can perform $C_j := C_j + 1$, for all $j \neq i$.

So long as there are no failures, each C_i will receive the same number of increments and it is clear that all will converge to the same value. However, it will be necessary to distinguish between certain identical values: the strict order is defined by or on the pairs (C_i, i), where i is the number of the site:

$$(C_i, i) < (C_j, j) \textit{ if } C_i < C_j \textit{ or } (C_i = C_j \textit{ and } i < j)$$

Kaneko [Kaneko 79] has proposed a variant of this method which limits the discrepancy between any pair of clocks to 1 at all times.

Lamport [Lamport 78] suggests that clocks should be incremented only after a necessary exchange of information between sites: site S_i increments its clock C_i between two successive local events. Further, when S_i sends a message it stamps it with the value of its clock C_i; the receiving site corrects its own clock if it is running late with respect to the time-stamp, increments it and then considers the event 'receipt of message'.

Figure 7 illustrates the working of Lamport's algorithm; here, the symbol ⤳ represents the sending of a message, and the resulting total order is:

$$a_1 \ b_1 \ c_1 \ a_2 \ c_2 \ a_3 \ a_4 \ b_2 \ a_5 \ b_3 \ c_3 \ c_4 \ b_4$$

This order differs from the true chronological order: a_1, b_1 and c_1 are really simultaneous events but have been put in serial order, and c_2, although occurring later than b_2, is placed before it. However, cause-and-effect relations are respected, whether between events on the same site or resulting from exchanges of messages between different sites.

Failures can have different effects on different algorithms; each algorithm has its own methods of handling these, requiring:

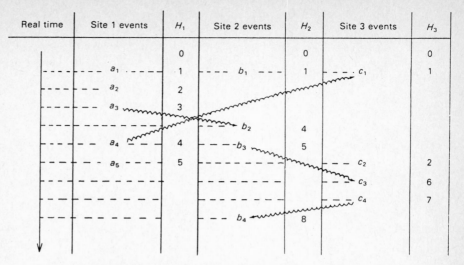

Fig. 7. *Management of clocks: Lamport's algorithm.*

(1) that the withdrawal of a site does not stop the normal incrementing of clocks on the other sites (only Kaneko [Kaneko 79] must perform special actions to deal with this problem);

(2) that a site can be restored dynamically after repair. This assumes that on restoration the site's clock can be re-set to a value which is consistent with those of the sites which remained active. It is easy with the Lamport method.

We shall consider logical clocks again in the examples at the end of this chapter.

4.3. Principles of distributed control

A number of requirements become clear when implementing algorithms for distributed control; these make it necessary to establish an ordering among the events of the system and the treatment in the preceding section provides us with a means for doing so. We now study some basic techniques for implementing distributed control.

The present state of the art on distributed systems does not provide a systematic method for translating an abstract synchronization expression into statements concerning local controllers and communication between them; we shall attempt, therefore, to derive some general principles. It should be remembered that the abstract expressions with which we are concerned define, apart from the synchronization points:

(1) a set E of variables which describe the state of the system,

(2) a set of conditions, which are functions of these state variables and which govern passage through the synchronization points,

(3) the changes to be made to the state variables as the system evolves.

4.3.1. Approximate representation of state variables

Distribution of the abstract expression means first of all that a representation of the state of the system has to be constructed, using local variables belonging to each controller. There are three main techniques by which this can be done:

— replication of set E: actual variables are set up at each site, corresponding to the complete set E and having the same meaning as the 'abstract' variables;

— distribution of set E: the set is separated into disjoint parts E_i, to each of which corresponds a set of actual variables at a single site;

— decomposition of the variables of E: each abstract variable is decomposed into a number of variables which are then located at different sites. An abstract variable is then a function of local variables.

A point of fundamental importance here is that the correspondence thus established between the abstract variables and their local representations is valid only so long as there is no activity in the system. In normal working the consequence of the delays introduced by the transmission of items of information is that the local variables often give only an *approximate* representation of the true state of the system.

The example given in section 4.1.2 illustrates how the partition of set E should be carried out: here, the variables *start(prod)* and *start(cons)* can be distributed respectively on sites 1 and 2. On the other hand, *finish (prod)* and *finish (cons)* must be replicated and one copy is always a delayed image of the original abstract variable.

4.3.2. Strengthening the abstract conditions

Since the abstract variables forming set E are to be represented by local variables, the abstract conditions governing passage through synchronization points and the modification of the state variables must be expressed in terms of these local variables. The conditions actually applied will not, in general, be identical to the abstract conditions because the local variables will be only either an approximate or a partial representation of the abstract variables. One way of handling the situation is to replace, at each site i, the abstract condition, which we shall call *CONDITION*, by a **local condition** *condition$_i$* involving only local variables and constructed so as to take account of the relation between the abstract and local variables. In order to maintain the approximate representation of abstract variables by local variables the controllers must cooperate to ensure that at all times and for all i:

condition$_i$ $\Rightarrow$ *CONDITION*

from which it follows that local conditions are never weaker than abstract conditions.

The methods by which local conditions may be formulated are too dependent on the characteristics of particular problems for any general principles to be established. However, two types of object, queues and counters, are very often involved in the expression of abstract conditions and in sections 4.4 and 4.5 we shall study their use in control algorithms. But, before doing so, we shall consider a simple example to illustrate two important points concerning allocation of resources.

4.3.3. Example

This example concerns access to a single resource. The state of this resource is represented by a Boolean variable *FREE* and access to the resource is bounded by two synchronization points *REQ (request)* and *REL (release)*: passage through *REQ* is conditional on *FREE* being **true**, after which it becomes **false**, returning to **true** only after passage through *REL*. This can be expressed as follows:

- $E = \{\textbf{\textit{Boolean}}\ FREE\}$
- synchronization points = $\{REQ,\ REL\}$
- abstract conditions: *condition* (*REQ*): *FREE*
  condition (*REL*): **true**
- update E: for *REQ*:   *FREE* := **false**
  for *REL*:   *FREE* := **true**

This controller can be implemented with the aid of a control message, which we call **privilege,** circulating around the processes organized in a virtual ring as in section 4.1.2. The approximate representations of the state variables on site i are then as follows:

(i) a Boolean $free_i$, set to **false** after any process at the site has occupied the resource, and to **true** otherwise;

(ii) a Boolean $priv_i$, set to **true** when site i is privileged, and to **false** otherwise.

The local conditions are then:

$condition_i$ (*REQ*): $priv_i$ **and** $free_i$
$condition_i$ (*REL*): **true**

The approximate representation is maintained as follows:

- for *REQ*: $free_i$:= **false**, *retain privilege*
- for *REL*: $free_i$:= **true**, *transmit privilege*
- after receiving privilege: $priv_i$:= **true**
- after transmiting privilege: $priv_i$:= **false**

Two remarks need to be made here.

(1) The local conditions on *REQ* are stronger than the abstract local

condition: the resource may be free but access may not be possible because the site may not yet be privileged. However, this ensures that no site is permanently denied access to the resource, because it will receive the privilege message within a finite time.

(2) Since $FREE = \cup\ free_i$ we have in fact broken down the state variable.

4.4. Replication of queues

We saw in chapter 2, section 3 that it is often convenient to use queues to solve problems of fairness and priority. Some distributed algorithms, e.g. those of Lamport [Lamport 78] and Herman [Herman 79], use a set of queues, one for each local controller, and service messages to maintain coherence; these can all be regarded as copies of a single abstract queue. We now use an example concerning mutual exclusion to demonstrate a method for **replication of queues** which can be adapted to other problems; this adaptation is illustrated in section 4.9.

4.4.1. Abstract expression for the problem

We consider the sharing of a single resource among a set of processes, in which only one process at a time may occupy the resource and may do so for only a finite time. The algorithm must satisfy these conditions:

  C1: Access by only one process at any time is guaranteed
  C2: Requests for access are dealt with fairly

For the second condition we set up a FIFO queue Q: requests are then dealt with in the order in which they are received. The abstract expression for the problem is then as follows.

(1) Synchronization points: REQ_k (process k requests the resource);
$\qquad\qquad\qquad\qquad\qquad\ \ REL_k$ (process k releases the resource).

(2) Set E: **queue**, Q (organized as stated, holding the markers REQ_k).

(3) Condition *condition* (REQ_k): REQ_k is at the head of Q.

(4) Processing of E: process k makes its request, REQ_k is put into the
$\qquad\qquad\qquad$ queue;
$\qquad\qquad\qquad$ process k issues REL_k, REQ_k is removed from the
$\qquad\qquad\qquad$ head of the queue.

This satisfies the required conditions because:

(C1) only one marker can be at the head of the queue at any one time, so only one process can access the resource at any one time;

(C2) the method of operating the queue ensures fairness.

4.4.2. Organization of the system

We consider a distributed system which conforms to the conditions given in section 4.1.1, with a single process P_i implemented at each site S_i. We assume that some system for time-stamping is provided, and the treatment to be developed will apply whatever the actual method used; in the absence of a single physical clock, condition C2 must be interpreted in terms of a logical clock (as described in section 4.2).

4.4.3. The algorithm [Ricart 81]

The abstract queue Q is replicated, so that at each site S_i there is a queue q_i holding the markers REQ_k.

As a first approach, we look for a method for processing Q which is as natural as possible:

(1) At site k, when process P_k arrives at the point REQ_k, the marker is put into the local queue q_k and a message $<REQ_k, t>$ is broadcast to all the other sites, where t is the (logical) time at which the request is made.

(2) At site i, when this message is received, marker REQ_k is put into queue q_i. The aim is that the q_i shall all be images, possibly delayed, of the abstract queue Q; because of the variable delays experienced by the different messages, a FIFO organization of the q_i is inappropriate, so the decision is to deal with these in increasing order of the time-stamps in the doublets $<REQ_k, t>$.

(3) When the process at site k arrives at the point REL_k, a message $<REL_k, t>$ is broadcast to all the other sites, which can then remove the corresponding marker from their queues q_i.

We now have to determine the local conditions (which will ensure that conditions C1 and C2 are satisfied); the requirement is that the request for access to the resource by the local process will be granted if it has been outstanding for longer than any of the other requests still waiting:

$$condition_i\,(REQ_i) = <REQ_i,\, t> \text{ is at the head of queue } q_i \qquad (1)$$
$$\textbf{and}$$
$$\textit{site}_i \text{ has received, from all other sites, messages time-stamped later than } t$$

The second part of this condition is intended to prevent the allocation of the resource in a situation such as that represented by Fig. 8.

Since the messages cannot overtake one another on the point-to-point channels, if site 1 had received any message whatever from site 2, time-stamped 7, it would be certain that all earlier messages from that site had already been received and, therefore, that a message such as $<REQ_2, 4>$ could not be in transit.

Condition (1) can be expressed more simply if the release markers are retained in the local queues. Assuming that initially every process sends a release message, the condition becomes:

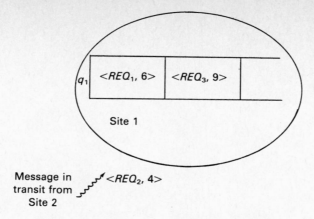

Fig. 8. *The request from Site 2, time-stamped 4, should be serviced before that from Site 1.*

$$condition_i\ (REQ_i) = <REQ_i,\ t>\ is\ at\ the\ head\ of\ q_i \qquad (2)$$

In the situation of Fig. 8, the queue q_1 is as follows:

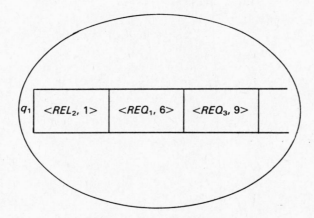

and the resource cannot be allocated to P_1, whether or not there is a message $<REQ_2,\ 4>$ in transit.

To avoid permanent denial of service to a process, as could happen in this case if P_2 had finished executing, or even excessively long waits, messages of the form $<REL_k,\ t>$ can be issued in response to requests, and are dealt with as follows:

When site 1 receives the message $<REQ_k,\ t>$, there are two possibilities:

(a) there is an unsatisfied request $<REQ_i,\ t'>$ with $t' < t$: site i then *delays* its response until it has accessed and then released the resource;

(b) there is no earlier request from site i, so the message $<REL_i, t''>$ is sent to site k. The system for time-stamping ensures that $t < t''$, consequently REQ_k can move up the queue in q_k.

Note: In [Ricart 81] a process which releases the resource sends the message REL only to those sites from which it has received requests. The cost corresponding to a request for the resource is therefore:

$N - 1$ request messages (sent out by the requesting site);

plus $N - 1$ messages advising release (which must be received before the resource can be accessed).

This is the minimum cost under the present assumptions. Carvalho [Carvalho 81] provides an optimized method which gives $2(N - 1)$ as the upper limit for the cost, but which requires a special interpretation of condition C2: some priorities are introduced dynamically, but do not lead to starvation.

4.4.4. Replication of the queues

This example has made use of certain general principles according to which the abstract queue Q can be replicated; these are illustrated by condition (1) of section 4.4.2:

(a) the time-stamping system ensures that the order in which requests are put into the local queues is the same for all sites: this is the first part of the condition.

(b) the abstract condition is strengthened in order to compensate for the uncertainties in specifying the actual state of the system, such as the possibility of messages in transit: this is the second part of the condition.

The application of this technique is illustrated in section 4.9.

4.5. Decomposition of monotonically increasing counters

Ideally, we wish to develop implementation techniques which could be applied to any abstract expression, but it is clear that the state of the art is not yet up to this. However, Carvalho [Carvalho 82] has developed general principles for dealing with some simple abstract expressions. We shall describe in this section Herman's method [Herman 81] for distributing a subset of the control modules described in chapter 2, section 2.3.

4.5.1. The abstract expression language

Following on from chapter 2, section 2.3, we choose a subset of control modules, retaining only $\# perm(P)$ and $\# term(P)$ of the five counters initially associated with each control procedure P. This choice clearly restricts the class of problems we shall be able to treat, but it will still include three classical problems: allocation of a resource of which there are M copies, the producer/consumer problem dealt with in section 4.1.2 and the reader/writer problem.

Example 1: resource with several copies, all equally accessible

The abstract condition can be written:

$$condition(U) = \# \, perm(U) - \# \, term(U) < M$$

where U is the procedure which operates on any of the M copies.

Example 2: reader/writer problem [Courtois 71]

The procedures to be controlled are R (read) and W (write); the abstract expressions are:

$$condition(R) = \# \, perm(W) - \# \, term(W) < 1$$
$$condition(W) = \# \, perm(W) - \# \, term(W) + \# \, perm(R)$$
$$- \# \, term(R) < 1$$

In both these examples, the condition for permission to start a process P has the form:

$$condition(P) = \sum_i \# \, perm(P_i) - \sum_k \# \, term(P_k) < C \qquad (1)$$

We take this form as a working hypothesis in what follows.

4.5.2. Organization of the system

To distribute control we implement, at each site i, a local controller CTL_i which manages the approximation to the state of the system. In order to manage this system, the controllers are linked logically in a virtual communication ring, each being able to send a message to its successor in the ring and to receive a message from its predecessor.

4.5.3. General principles

First, as an informal introductory example, consider the managing of a bank account by two people A and B, each with a cheque book. The constraint imposed by the bank is that the condition:

total withdrawals to date — total deposits to date $\leqslant 0$

is satisfied after every withdrawal.

A and B meet from time to time to compare notes, or exchange letters, but for most of the time each wishes to act independently of the other in managing his or her finances.

Suppose that A knows exactly his total withdrawals and deposits but can only estimate those of B; if these numbers always satisfy the inequalities:

A's estimate of B's deposits $\leqslant$ *total of B's actual deposits*

and

A's estimate of B's withdrawals $\geqslant$ *total of B's actual withdrawals*

then A can be certain that a withdrawal made by him will not overdraw the account, provided that he checks that this does not violate the condition:

total of A's withdrawals + *estimate of B's withdrawals*
− total of A's deposits − estimate of B's deposits < *0*

Analogously, for every process P we provide every local controller with estimates of the numbers of permissions and terminations of execution of P recorded by all the other controllers. From the form of condition (1) of section 4.5.1, we see that these estimates must be at the upper bound for the permissions and the lower bound for the terminations.

Before going any further, we should explain the notation we shall use.

(1) Capitals are used for the counters in the abstract expressions: thus, $PERM(P)$ for $\#\ perm(P)$.

(2) Lower-case letters are used for local variables, with a suffix to define the site.

(3) u is used to indicate an upper bound, l a lower bound.

(4) The suffix i denotes the site currently under consideration, k the others.

In the above example, the total of the withdrawals from the account is made up of an amount from A and an amount from B, each known (exactly) locally and estimated elsewhere. Similarly, in order to distribute control, each counter (for permission or termination) will be broken down into as many local counters as there are sites. For example, the local counter $perm_i(P)$ gives the number of permissions to execute the process P issued by CTL_i. Thus we have:

$$\sum_i perm_i(P) = PERM(P)$$
$$\sum_i term_i(P) = TERM(P)$$

If, for each counter $PERM(P)$ and for each site S_i, we can construct an upper bound $u.perm_i(P)$ for the sum of the local counter $perm_i(P)$ at the other sites, and similarly for $TERM(P)$ a lower bound $l.term_i$ for the sum of the local counters $term_k(P)$, we can construct a local condition stronger than any abstract condition of the form (1). This will be expressed in terms of the local counters, together with the local upper and lower bounds.

Thus, for example 1 of section 4.5, the abstract condition:

$$CONDITION(U) = PERM(U) - TERM(U) < M$$

can be replaced by the local condition:

$$condition_i(U) = perm_i(U) + u.perm_i(U) - (term_i(U) + l.term_i(U)) < M$$

Clearly, at any site S_i, we need only implement what is strictly necessary for the control of the local processes: there is no obligation to handle all possible conditions, counters and bounds.

When the form (1) imposed on the conditions is taken into account, the following lemma is self-evident.

LEMMA

If the upper and lower bounds have been correctly constructed in the sense that they always satisfy the inequalities:

$$l.term_i(P) \leqslant \sum_{k \neq i} term_k(P) \tag{3}$$

$$u.perm_i(P) \geqslant \sum_{k \neq i} perm_k(P) \tag{4}$$

for all i, then for every site S_i:

$$condition_i(P) \Rightarrow condition\ (P)$$

The local controller gives permission for execution of a controlled process only when the relevant local condition is satisfied; the lemma guarantees that this distribution of control really is an implementation of the abstract synchronization condition.

4.5.4. Management of approximate representations

We now take up the question of constructing the upper and lower bounds, assuming there are no system failures.

MANAGEMENT OF LOWER BOUNDS

Returning for the moment to the bank-account example of section 4.5.3, suppose B sends A a statement of his (B's) deposits. Because of the delays in transmission, the information received by A may not give a correct picture of what B has paid into the account, but for A's purpose it will always be at worst an under-estimate and therefore satisfactory.

It is clear that values for the variables $l.term_i(P)$ can be generated by an analogous process. The principle is simple:

— each time the counter $term_i(P)$ is increased, the local controller CTL_i sends a message $<+ l.term(P), i>$ to increment the lower bounds;

— when site i receives a message $<+ l.term(P), k>$, where $k \neq i$, it increments its own lower bound $l.term_i(P)$ and returns the message to the ring.

Thus, at every instant:

$$l.term_i(P) = \sum_{k \neq i} (term_k(P) - \text{number of messages} <+ l.term(P), k>$$
$$\text{in transit between } k \text{ and } i) \tag{3a}$$

which suffices for invariant (3) above. At the start-up of the system, variables $term_i(P)$ and $l.term_i(P)$ are initialized to zero.

Continuing with the producer/consumer problem of section 4.1.2 and assuming that the production and consumption processes are implemented on sites 1 and 2 respectively, we see that the variables and the local conditions can be written as in Table 1.

Table 1

Site	Approximate representation	Local condition
1	$perm_1(PROD)$, $term_1(PROD)$ $l.term_1(CONS)$	$condition_1(PROD) =$ $perm_1(PROD) - l.term_i(CONS) < N$
2	$perm_2(CONS)$, $term_2(CONS)$ $l.term_2(PROD)$	$condition_2(CONS) =$ $perm_2(CONS) - l.term_2(PROD) < 0$

Note: The aim of flow control in a communication network or on a point-to-point lane is to limit the rate at which the transmitter generates messages to a rate the receiver can handle. Considered in the abstract, this synchronization problem, which *by its very nature* is not amenable to central control (this is obvious in the case of a two-point lane), is in fact the producer/consumer problem and the variables in Table 1 can be seen to be equivalent to those of the flow-control problem. Thus:

$perm_1(PROD)$ is the serial number of the last message sent out or being sent out;

$l.term_1(CONS)$ is the serial number of the last acknowledgement received.

MANAGEMENT OF UPPER BOUNDS

The management of upper bounds is more difficult. In the bank-account example, A's needs will not be satisfied by delayed information concerning B's withdrawals; but if B has sent a message to A saying that for the time being he does not expect to withdraw more than a certain amount, then A can use this as an estimate of B's total withdrawals. B can act independently of A so long as he stays within this limit; but if he wishes to exceed it, he must inform A and wait for a response — which could be simply an acknowledgement of receipt of the message. The requirement to wait for a response ensures that two withdrawals made simultaneously by A and B would not overdraw the account. It may be impossible to make any further withdrawals, in which case one of the partners must cancel any request he was intending to make and wait until the financial situation improves.

Note that in this transaction B waits for A's response, not for his **agreement**: a formal acknowledgement of receipt of the message, provided by the postal or telecommunications authority, will suffice. This is clearly satisfactory so long as the financial position is sound; A need only record the new information concerning B's activities and need not go to the trouble of drafting a reply. On the other hand, a conflict of interests will cause the system to slow down: circuits will at first be increased for both partners, but further withdrawals will then be prohibited.

It should be noted that the quantitative relations in a problem can influence the distribution of control. If there are frequent conflicts of interest the cost of control operations should not be attributed to the method used for distributing the control, but rather to the concept of distributed control itself; because, in such circumstances, the various processes — in this example, the holders of the account — are not really autonomous. Centralized control would seem preferable here.

When a conflict of interests arises in the bank-account example, we do not wish this to result in both A and B cancelling their requests. There is no need for a lengthy dialogue to be embarked on to resolve the conflict, because it is simply a matter of making sure that the decisions taken by the two parties are consistent; a possible solution is that the second of the two requests recorded is the one to be cancelled. Here, again, real or universal time is not relevant: a postal franking mark will suffice, with an agreed bias, say in favour of A, to resolve the ambiguity if both marks show the same time.

We can use these principles to guide us in constructing upper bounds. With each local counter $perm_i(P)$ we associate a variable $max.perm_i(P)$, called the local limit, which represents the amount of freedom allowed to $perm_i(P)$ as the system evolves. More precisely, if $max.perm_i(P) - perm_i(P) = c$, the controller S_i undertakes not to allow more than c further executions of P in the near future. We say that CTL_i has a **credit** of c permissions for procedure P. Service messages then ensure that $u.perm_i(P)$ is almost a true image of $\sum_{k \neq i} max.perm_k(P)$.

(a) Increasing the local limits

This first type of service message allows the controllers to increase their local limits (granting credit). The procedure is as follows:

(1) S_i sends the message $<+u.perm(P), i>$.

(2) On receiving this message, each site S_k increments $u.perm_k(P)$ by 1 and returns the message to the ring.

(3) When the message returns to S_i after a complete circuit of the ring, every local bound $u.perm_k(P)$ will have been increased by 1; S_i can then increment its own local limit $max.perm_i(P)$.

This method for generating upper bounds involves the risk of deadlock of the system: thus, in Example 1 of section 4.5.1, it could happen that, as a consequence of too many increases having been made to local limits, all the $u.perm_i(P)$ are greater than R, so that no further permissions can be issued. There is therefore a need for a protocol allowing for local limits to be decreased.

(b) Decreasing the local limits

The decrease of a local limit by controller CTL_i is brought about as follows:

(1) If the limit at site S_i can be reduced, i.e. if $perm_i(P) < max.perm_i(P)$, S_i makes the decrement and *then* puts the message $<- u.perm(P), i>$ onto the ring.

(2) As this message circulates round the ring, each site S_k decrements $u.perm_k(P)$ and hands the message on to its successor.

(3) When the message has travelled all round the ring, site S_i removes it.

This provision makes it possible to avoid deadlock; a full treatment of this problem involves a lengthy analysis and it seems preferable to study the question as it arises in particular problems. We shall therefore simply give a sketch of the principles underlying a general method — to show that a solution exists — from which some methods for attacking particular cases can be deduced.

Deadlock would result from there being several conflicting demands to increase local limits; to avoid this, all but one of the demands must be cancelled (if all are cancelled there is a risk of starting an endless cycle of increases and reductions). To achieve this, every message is given a time-stamp and every controller keeps a trace of all the requests for incrementation which it receives, together with these logical timings. Because of the possibility of cancellations, there must be provision for messages to suppress recordings of requests in the traces. Whenever a conflict seems possible, each local controller examines its trace to see if this includes any demands for increases which are time-stamped earlier than its own demands and, if there are any such demands, sets in motion a systematic reduction of its own local limits. The credits thus cancelled are restored, with their original logical timings, when they reach the head of the trace.

The practical difficulties here are:

— in determining that there is a conflict: one criterion could be that conflict is possible when all the local conditions have remained false for too long;

— in the methods for processing the traces (messages cancelling records of requests).

In our view, it would be a bad decision to adopt a standard method for dealing with the second issue, because this would be equivalent to assuming that there is in fact a conflict. The special conditions and the quantitative aspects of particular problems usually make it possible to devise a simpler treatment.

GENERAL PRINCIPLES

The method by which the upper bounds are generated implies that at all times:

$$u.perm_i(P) = \sum_{k \neq i} (max.perm_k(P)$$

+ number of $<+ u.perm(P), k>$ in transit between i and k
+ number of $<- u.perm(P), k>$ in transit between k and i) (4a)

and therefore that:

$$u.perm_i(P) \geq \sum_{k \neq i} max.perm_k(P) \qquad (4b)$$

Since, also, $max.perm_k(P) \geq perm_k(P)$ by definition, it follows that:

$$u.perm_i(P) \geq \sum_{k \neq i} perm_k(P)$$

which is the inequality (4) required by the lemma described in section 4.5.3. The other inequality (3) having already been established, it follows that the lemma holds, provided that the variables $perm_i(P)$, $u.perm_i(P)$ and $max.perm_i(P)$ are set to zero when the system is started. This in turn proves that the procedures for distributing control are functioning correctly.

Example

For the management of a resource for which there are R equally available instances, we implement at each site the variables $perm_i(U)$, $max.perm_i(U)$, $u.perm_i(U)$, $term_i(U)$ and $l.term_i(U)$.

The local conditions are:

$$condition_i(U) = perm_i(U) + u.perm_i(U) - term_i(U) - l.term_i(U) < R$$

and

$$perm_i(U) < max.perm_i(U)$$

Table 2

Message received	Cause	Actions resulting
$<+ l.term(P), k \neq i>$	increment $term_k(P)$	$l.term_i(P) := l.term_i(P) + 1$; output to the ring
$<+ u.perm(P), k \neq i>$	increment $max.perm_k(P)$	$u.perm_i(P) := u.perm_i(P) + 1$; output to the ring
$<- u.perm(P), k \neq i>$	decrement $max.perm_k(P)$	$u.perm_i(P) := u.perm_i(P) - 1$; output to the ring
	increment $term_i(P)$	output $<+ u.term(P), i>$
	wish to increment $max.perm_i(P)$	output $<+ u.perm(P), i>$
	wish to decrement $max.perm_i(P)$	$max.perm_i(P) := max.perm_i(P) - 1$; output $<- u.perm(P), i>$
$<+ l.term(P), i>$	complete turn of ring	
$<+ u.perm(P), i>$	complete turn	$max.perm_i(P) := max.perm_i(P) + 1$;
$<- u.perm(P), i>$	complete turn	

The service messages received or sent by site S_i, together with the processing associated with these, are summarized in Table 2.

4.6. Conclusion

There are a number of different ways in which the synchronization constraints on a distributed system can be implemented.

(1) By means of a single controller. This has advantages in certain cases because the techniques for central control have now been fully mastered and the approach correspondingly simplified. Use of this method is justified when, for example, there is only one resource to be allocated or when using a single controller does not give rise to further problems of time-constraints or reliability.

(2) By means of distributed controllers. Various considerations, such as distributed resources or constraints on access times, may make it necessary to implement a number of controllers distributed over the system. Their actions must be coordinated so that the abstract synchronization condition for the complete system is obeyed, and for this there are several solutions:

(a) Reproduce the conditions of a centralized allocation of resources by imposing the condition that only one controller may operate at any one time. This is not a satisfactory solution since it fails to take advantage of the fact that control has been distributed. Implementing mutual exclusion may prove to be costly. It can be adopted when the need for multiple controllers is imposed from outside the system or, for reasons of reliability, when the mutual exclusion algorithm can deal with failures.

(b) Abandon the concept of mutual exclusion and use the two basic methods described in the preceding sections to implement a truly distributed system of control:

(i) By using several copies of the control information. Coherence among these copies is ensured by the protocols governing cooperation between controllers, and as a consequence of the possibility of establishing a total ordering among the system events.

(ii) By using partial or approximate representation of the control information. The resulting uncertainty in the knowledge of the state of the system is compensated for by the use of local conditions which are stronger than the abstract condition for the system as a whole. The extent of this uncertainty cannot, however, be arbitrary, and negotiations between the controllers are introduced to limit it. Here, again, the concept of order can be useful in setting priorities among the actions of the controllers.

The choice of method in any given case depends on the particular constraints imposed, relating, for example, to time, reliability or the kind of distribution adopted. In evaluating the various possibilities, account must be taken of the number of messages to be exchanged, the relative independence of the controllers and — in the interest of minimizing the risk of errors — the simplicity of the control algorithm.

4.7. Illustration 1: circulation and regeneration of the privilege message on a virtual ring

We have shown on several occasions (e.g. sections 4.1.2, 4.2, 4.3.3) that a set of distributed processes can be controlled by the use of a special message which we have called **privilege**. There are two problems:

(i) how to cause the message to circulate among the different sites so as to ensure equitability of treatment,

(ii) how to avoid total stoppage of the system if the message is lost, and how to maintain its integrity?

We now give some possible solutions to these problems.

To decide on a routing for **privilege,** we consider the sites as being arranged on a communications ring, with communication in one direction only and such that each site can communicate only with a neighbour.

Suppose we have a network of N sites, completely linked (physically or logically). Each site is permanently labelled with a number between 0 and $N-1$. Consequently, each site has a successor or neighbour to the right, and a predecessor or neighbour to the left. For the site labelled i, we denote the labels for its neighbours as R_i and L_i respectively, and when the system is operating normally, we have

$$R_i = i \oplus 1 \ (mod \ N), \ L_i = i \ominus 1 \ (mod \ N)$$

because of the **virtual ring** arrangement.

Privilege is expressed by a particular combination of the state variables, and its mode of circulation around the virtual ring is determined by one of two algorithms elaborated by Mossière [Mossière 77] and Le Lann [Le Lann 78] respectively, both adaptations of a method proposed by Dijkstra [Dijkstra 74]; the principle on which these are based is described in the next section. The proper functioning of these algorithms in case of failure of a site depends on the possibility of reconfiguring the ring. No problem is posed by the removal of a site, provided that this does not compromise the entire network: it is simply a question of updating the neighbours R_i and L_i. We are not concerned here with the management of the ring, which is discussed in [Le Lann 77], and we assume that updating takes place automatically; we are, however, interested in the problem of maintaining the integrity of **privilege**.

4.7.1. Principle of the algorithm

Suppose that on each site i there is a process P_i which is responsible for the circulation of **privilege,** and that the following conditions hold:

(1) With each of these N processes is associated a state variable $S[i]$ which can take integer values between 0 and $K-1$.

(2) Each variable $S[i]$ is accessible to its 'owner' P_i and can be read by its successor process P_{R_i}.

(3) P_i is **privileged** when $S[i] \neq S[L_i]$ for $i \neq 0$
$$S[0] = S[L_0] \quad \text{otherwise}$$

(4) A **privileged** process gives up its **privilege** after a finite time, by changing state:

$$S[i] := S[L_i] \qquad\qquad \text{if } i \neq 0$$
$$S[0] := S[0] + 1(mod\ K) \qquad\qquad \text{otherwise}$$

(5) There is no other means by which a process can change its state.

P_i can determine if it is in the **privileged** state by either of two methods:

- by testing the state variable of its predecessor $S[L_i]$ [Mossière 77];
- by waiting until its predecessor sends a special message carrying the value of $S[L_i]$, signalling that it is transferring **privilege** to P_i [Le Lann 77].

Example

If $K = 2$ and if the initial state of the system is 000, it passes through the states:

$$\overset{*}{0}00 - \overset{*}{1}00 - 1\overset{*}{1}0 - 11\overset{*}{1} - 0\overset{*}{1}1 - 00\overset{*}{1}$$

where the '*' identifies the state variable of the **privileged** process.

Here we give only a very informal demonstration of the way in which the algorithm works; its validity is proved in [Mossière 77].

Figure 9 shows how the system for this example changes through time. The transfer of **privilege** can be regarded as the advance of a wavefront, shown as a dotted line, across the diagram; it disappears when the state represented by Fig. 9d is reached, and is then regenerated because of the asymmetrical character of P_0.

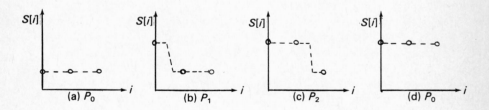

Fig. 9. *Evolution of state variables (the process indicated has the **privilege**).*

4.7.2. Removal and restoration of a process

Here we shall study the consequences first of removing one of the processes and then of restoring a process which has been removed [Mossière 77].

REMOVAL OF A PROCESS OTHER THAN P_0

A study of Fig. 9 makes it clear that this causes neither the disappearance nor the creation of **privilege**: no new front is created. The only cases in which the front disappears are those corresponding to the loss of P_2 in Fig. 9c, but, in these cases, P_0 regenerates a new front as before.

REMOVAL OF P_0

This makes it impossible to regenerate the front at the end of the cycle (Fig. 9d); however, it is important to note that the principle of mutual exclusion is not invalidated.

A solution to this problem can be found in which P_0 is replaced by another process: on a ring, the process which must play the role of P_0 is the only one for which $L_i > i$. Every process must therefore make provision for this possibility [Mossière 77]:

> **if** $L_i > i$ **then** $<$ *behave as* $P_0 >$
>   **else** $<$ *behave as* $P_i >$ **endif**

In the treatment of the problem by Le Lann [Le Lann 78], it is necessary to know, whenever the ring has to be reconfigured, if the failure which has resulted in the breaking of the ring has also caused a loss of **privilege**. To provide this information, the process P_i responsible for the reconfiguration interrogates its new left-hand neighbour; **privilege** has been lost if

$$L_i > i \text{ and } S[L_i] = S[i]$$

or

$$L_i < i \text{ and } S[L_i] \neq S[i]$$

P_i regenerates **privilege** and sets, respectively:

$$S[i] := S[i] + 1 \pmod{N}$$

or

$$S[i] := S[L_i]$$

RESTORATION OF A PROCESS

In order to restore itself, the process i must re-initialize $S[i]$. Provided that no reading of $S[j]$, the state variable of site $j=R_i$, has been authorized during the time when it is in the critical section, it is sufficient if P_i sets $S[i]$ as follows:

if $R_i < i$ **then** $S[i] := S[R_i] - 1$
    else $S[i] := S[R_i]$
endif

4.8. Illustration 2: processes competing for resources — the car park problem

As an illustration of competition between processes for limited resources, let us consider the problem of managing a car park. The processes are the cars and the resources they compete for are the parking spaces. Each process can be represented by the sequence of events:

e: entering
p: parking
l: leaving

If we denote by $\#e$ and $\#l$ the number of e-events and l-events, respectively, that have occurred, the abstract expression for the synchronization constraint is

$$\#e - \#l \le N \tag{1}$$

where N is the total number of parking spaces available.
    Note that the condition

$$\#e \ge \#l \tag{2}$$

is satisfied by definition and requires no specific control.
    To implement expression (1) we use the variables E and L to represent the values of the counters $\#e$ and $\#l$ respectively. The controller must cause the following actions to be taken at the synchronization points e and l:

A_e: *wait until* $E - L < N$; $E := E + 1$
A_l: $L := L + 1$

If several processes arrive simultaneously at a synchronization point, e.g. at l, the controller must ensure that the actions A_e are mutually consistent. This can be done by causing these actions to be performed in a mutually exclusive manner, i.e. serially; and similarly for point e. On the other hand, A_e and A_l are independent. This is not the case, however, if we make the change of variable:

$$Y = N - E + L \tag{3}$$

which gives the number of free spaces in the car park, because the controller's actions are now:

A'_e: *wait until* $Y > 0$; $Y := Y - 1$
A'_l: $Y := Y + 1$

The mutual exclusion or serialization must now be imposed on the complete set of actions, both at e and at l.

Note that the controller A_e'/A_l' can be represented by a process which is called by the competing processes — the cars — and which causes a single event e or l to occur. In contrast, a controller of the type A_e/A_l can be represented by a pair of independent processes, one performing the actions A_e in serial order and the other the actions A_l, also serially. These two processes cooperate by sharing the variable S, as is done in models of producer/consumer systems in common use.

If the system is implemented in a centralized way, with a single lane serving both as entry and exit, the events e and l are recorded in the variables E and L, respectively, or together in the variable Y. In this case, there is no difficulty in basing control on either of the models A_e/A_l or A_e'/A_l'. But, if this is done in a distributed manner — e.g. if there are two lanes — events e and l may not be observable on the same site, and abstract expression (1) can be implemented in either of two ways, as follows.

Centralized control: this is a trivial solution, consisting in bringing together onto a single site, all the variables and statements needed for synchronization. A single control process is imposed, to which all other processes at the various sites send messages. The situation is now exactly that of a centralized system, with little parallel operation and with reliability depending on the single privileged site, etc.

Distributed control: distributing control among p sites is equivalent to having p control processes. In the following sections we consider three types of solution to this problem:

(a) Sharing the variables in the abstract expression among the controllers.

(b) Partitioning these variables into p components.

(c) Replicating the variables, while maintaining consistency.

4.8.1. Shared variables

Suppose there are two lanes to the car park, one for entry and the other for exit. This is equivalent to stating that one controller (or attendant) records the number of entries $E = \#e$ at site 1, and another records the departures $L = \#l$ at site 2. An *a priori* condition for a car to be allowed to enter the car park, i.e. for the process to pass through synchronization point e, is:

$$E - L < N \tag{4}$$

The attendant at site 1, who must impose this condition, knows the value of E exactly, whilst the value of L is known exactly to the attendant at site 2, who must send this value to his colleague. Because of delays in transmission, attendant 1 will at any time have only a delayed image $\overline{L}$ of L, with $\overline{L} < L$; if therefore he checks that

$$E - \overline{L} < N \tag{5}$$

is satisfied, he can be certain that (4) is satisfied and that invariant (1) is respected.

This implementation is a good illustration of the method of distributing the monotonically-increasing counters described in section 4.1.2.

Note: The growth of the numbers E and L can be limited by recording these modulo some sufficiently large number K. In this example, $K = 2N$ is suitable, giving, for the expression of condition (4)

$$0 \leqslant E - L < N \text{ or } N < L - E \tag{6}$$

where E and L are taken modulo $2N$.

4.8.2. Partitioned variables

Suppose that the car park has p lanes, each allowing both entry and exit; if E_i and L_i are the total numbers of cars entering and leaving, respectively, recorded by the attendant at lane i, we have:

$$E = E_0 + E_1 + \dots E_{p-1}$$
$$L = L_0 + L_1 + \dots L_{p-1}$$

The methods developed in section 4.5 can be applied to the processing of these $2p$ values, but they result in a very complex algorithm and a need for the transmission of very large numbers of messages.

Alternatively, we can distribute the parking spaces among the controllers (attendants), giving each a 'credit' of Y_i available spaces. This initial distribution is modified in the course of events: some attendants may find that they have to refuse entry although there are free spaces (controlled by other attendants), a drawback which can be remedied by a periodic redistribution of the credits.

$$\text{Initially, } Y = \sum_{i=0}^{p} Y_i = N \tag{7}$$

Suppose the attendant at lane 1 transfers a credit R_i periodically to the attendant at lane $i \oplus 1$ (*mod p*). Then the number of free spaces is always given by:

$$Y = N - E + L = \sum_{i=1}^{p} (Y_i + R_i) \tag{8}$$

When the message R_i arrives at site $j = i \oplus 1$ (*mod p*), the attendant there increases his credit:

$$Y_j := Y_j + R_i$$

the attendant at site i having of course reduced his credit by this amount on sending the message.

When a car wishes to enter the car park through lane i, the attendant allows it to do so if $Y_i > 0$; otherwise, he waits until one or other of the following events occurs:

- a car leaves by this lane, in which case Y_i becomes $Y_i + 1$;
- a message of redistribution of credits arrives from his neighbour at site $k = i \ominus 1 \ (mod \ p)$, in which case Y_i becomes $Y_i + R_k$.

4.8.3. Maintenance of the consistency of a shared variable

A possible way in which cooperation between the attendants is achieved, is to ensure that only one of them has access to variable Y, giving the number of places available, at any one time. A simple way to do this is to arrange the lanes in a virtual ring, with each linked to a predecessor from which it receives messages and to a successor to which it sends messages (cf. section 4.2).

A first attempt at a solution uses the p attendants, one at each lane, and a runner. The latter goes round the ring from one attendant to the next, carrying the value of Y. If, when he arrives at a lane where there is a car waiting to enter, this value is positive, the car can be allowed to enter and the value is reduced by 1. Strictly, no car should be allowed to leave by any lane unless the runner is there, so that the value of Y can be increased appropriately. In fact, however, the attendant there can allow cars to leave, noting the number that do so and giving this number to the runner when he arrives. With this arrangement only one lane can provide entry at a time and the rate at which entries can be made is determined by the speed with which the runner goes round the ring. It might therefore be more efficient to designate just one particular lane as entry point as long, of course, as it is available. Any study of a solution must therefore be made in terms of the conditions imposed by the need to strike a balance between effectiveness and reliability.

In the method of solution just given, the order in which cars are allowed to enter the car park is set by the runner: it is not necessarily that in which they arrive at the entry points. Further, it does not guarantee that a waiting car will eventually be allowed to enter, for it could happen that the runner always arrives at this lane with a zero value for Y: so there is the possibility of an **infinite wait,** or **starvation.** There is therefore a need to devise a solution which is fair in the sense of guaranteeing that service will always be provided in a certain order. In a centralized system, this order is usually ensured by a mutual exclusion mechanism for access to the critical variable (here, Y), either by means of a single queue or, better, by use of the central clock. In a distributed system we need to define a **strict total ordering** (cf. sections 4.1.2, 4.2).

If such an ordering exists, each car is given a rank in this order when it arrives at a lane, whether for entry or exit. It is no longer necessary to circulate a single copy of variable Y in order to ensure consistency, because the ordering guarantees mutually exclusive access to Y. What is, of course, necessary for the establishment of the order is the existence of a protocol for communication between attendants, so the attendant dealing with the car ranked $i + 1$ knows when the car ranked i has been dealt with: as we have seen, a broadcast protocol can be used in such circumstances. For this, a copy of Y is held at each site. Immediately after allowing a car to enter or leave, an attendant **broadcasts** its rank to all his colleagues, together with the operation he has performed on variable Y. The attendant who can next perform any operation is the one who will deal with the next rank number.

In this example, it is clear that the exit operations need not be ordered; whenever a car wishes to leave, the attendant can allow it to do so, and broadcasts the message:

> *add 1 to Y*

The various copies of Y will not now remain strictly identical, but they will remain consistent. Let $Y_{(i)}$ be the value of Y held by the attendant at lane i; after allowing a car to enter, he will:

(record)	*subtract 1 from $Y_{(i)}$*
(broadcast)	*subtract 1 from Y, rank number*

Simultaneously, the attendant at site j may have allowed a car to leave, performing

(record)	*add 1 to $Y_{(j)}$*
(broadcast)	*add 1 to Y*

Thus, $Y_{(i)}$ will have been first reduced and then increased, whilst the reverse will have happened to $Y_{(j)}$. Either sequence could have operated on the other copies. Strict ordering of these operations is not necessary, because they are **commutative**. However, this is not always the case, as the following example [Cornafion 81] shows.

Suppose there are four attendants A, B, C and D, and that at instant $t = 0$ there are 100 free parking spaces; three of these attendants make various allocations and broadcast the following messages:

> M1: 20 more spaces are free,
> M2: 10 more spaces have been taken,
> M3: I am reserving 10% of the free spaces for cleaning.

Table 3 below shows that unless some constraint is placed on the order in which the various requests arrive at sites A, B, C and D, the four attendants will have inconsistent information. If each attendant keeps his own copy of the state of allocation of parking spaces, the different copies will be consister only if updating is done in the same order at each site.

Table 3

Order of arrival	Message	Free spaces	Message	Free spaces	Message	Free spaces	Message	Free spaces
0		100		100		100		100
1	M1	120	M1	120	M3	90	M2	90
2	M3	108	M2	110	M1	110	M3	81
3	M2	98	M3	99	M2	100	M1	101

4.9. Illustration 3: maintenance of consistency among copies of the same information

4.9.1. Analysis of the problem

Suppose we have an item of information F, such as a variable, a file, a data base, etc., to which access can be made by certain operations. For simplicity, we consider two types of operation:

WRITE: These are programs of greater or less complexity whose final effect is to modify the value of F. In particular, F can be read during the execution of a *WRITE*. The condition is imposed that *WRITE* is applied to the 'last version' of F.

CONSULT: The effect is to deliver a value of F, not necessarily up to date for all modifications.

The abstract conditions controlling permission to perform these operations are always satisfied for *CONSULT*, and impose mutually exclusive access among the *WRITE* operations.

For the sake of the reliability and speed of *CONSULT* operations, each of the N sites of the distributed system holds a copy, $COPY_i$, of F; the problem is to maintain consistency among these copies, which can be defined as follows:

Provided that no new *WRITE* operations are performed, all the $COPY_i$ must become identical within a finite time.

To achieve this, we need only require that the *WRITE* operations are performed in the same order at all sites, implying in particular that every WRITE is broadcast to all the sites: this avoids the need to impose the condition of mutually exclusive access to the sytem as a whole: each site can work at its own pace, so that at any instant the various $COPY_i$ can differ.

The order in which the *WRITE* operations are performed, which is the same for all sites, can be obtained by the method given in [Lamport 78], which we described in section 4.2. Lamport deals only with the maintenance of consistency, the effect of breakdowns being treated in detail in [Herman 79].

4.9.2. The algorithm

At each site i, a program $CLERK$ is responsible for the copy of F. This responds immediately to any $CONSULT$ call by delivering the current state of $COPY_i$. Processing the $WRITE$s requires cooperation among the $CLERK$s, which exchange messages which have this structure:

<*nature of message, parameters, time-stamp*>

A message can be, for example, the identifier of a $WRITE$ operation together with its parameters — we shall omit the latter in what follows; unless anything to the contrary is said, the time-stamp is the local time at which the message was sent. The message corresponding to a $WRITE$ will be denoted by (W, T), where T is the time-stamp.

The principle of the algorithm is this. Each $CLERK$ handles N FIFO queues of messages, one for each site including its own. There are these actions:

(1) *Recording of the WRITE operations:*
- when site i decides to perform a $WRITE$ operation, it broadcasts a message (W, T_i) to all sites, recording this in its queue;
- when site j receives this message, it adds it to its queue numbered i;
- the clocks are updated every time a message is received according to the procedure of Lamport.

(2) *Processing of the WRITE operations.* Each $CLERK$ works through its queues at its own pace, observing these conditions:
- it can only handle the messages at the heads of the queues;
- it cannot handle a message (W, T_k) unless the messages at the heads of all the other queues are time-stamped later than T_k.

The second of these conditions means that if the queue numbered j at site i is empty, no further processing can be performed at this site. In order to continue, $CLERK_i$ has the freedom to send to site j, **and only to that site,** a special enquiry message which $CLERK_j$ acknowledges immediately on receipt. $CLERK_i$ records this acknowledgement in its queue j, which therefore becomes replenished, after a finite interval, either with the acknowledgement message or by some other message which was in the course of transmission at the time of the enquiry.

This can be summarized by saying that three types of message are exchanged between the sites: W (write), ENQ (enquiry) and ACK (acknowledgement). The local operations at site i by $CLERK_i$ are therefore as in Table 4.

Table 4

Message	Reason for sending	Action on receipt: in all cases update clock and then...	Action after handling: (earliest time-stamp)
W_j	Site j wishes to write	Put message in queue number j	Carry out what is required and delete message
ENQ_j	Queue number i on site j is empty	Put message in queue j and send ACK_i to site j	Delete message
ACK_j	Response to enquiry	Put in queue	Delete message

4.10. Illustration 4: distributed algorithm for the prevention of deadlocks

This section shows how a distributed algorithm for the prevention of deadlocks in the allocation of resources, based on [Lomet 78], can apply the principle of state variable partitioning, described in section 4.5.

4.10.1. Analysis of the problem

Suppose there are K processes $P_1, P_2, \ldots P_K$, all of which can use any or all of the N resources $R_1, R_2, \ldots R_N$. The synchronization points for the system are:

GET_i: seize R_i
REL_i: release R_i

There is a **claim** for each process P_k which lists all the resources which it may need to use. Initially, nothing is known about the order in which these may be seized or released.

The state of the system is defined by the variables I_i and A_k, where:

I_i $(i = 1, N)$ is the number of the process which is using R_i at that instant, or 0 if R_i is not then being used

A_k $(k = 1, K)$ is the claim of process P_k

With these variables we can construct the graph of the relation $\mathcal{B}$ ('might-block'), defined as follows:

P_{k1} $\mathcal{B}$ P_{k2} *iff* $\exists R_i : I_i = k1$ *and* $R_i \in A_{k2}$

The corresponding arc of the graph is

$$P_{k1} \xrightarrow{\quad R_i \quad} P_{k2}$$

The abstract conditions for crossing the synchronization points are:

condition (GET_i): $I_i = 0$ **and** 'this allocation will not produce a
cycle in the graph of $\mathcal{B}$'   (1)

Consider now three processes using three resources according to the following pattern:

	P_1		P_2		P_3
(a)	GET_1	(b)	GET_2	(c)	GET_3
	GET_2		GET_3		GET_1
	REL_1		REL_3		REL_1
	REL_2		REL_2		REL_3

If the system evolves in such a way that points (a), (b) and (c) are encountered in this order, process P_3 will not be able to use resource R_3, for the moment it arrives at (c) the graph is:

$$P_2 \xrightarrow{\quad R_2 \quad} P_1 \xrightarrow{\quad R_1 \quad} P_3$$

If R_3 were then allocated to P_3, the corresponding arc:

$$P_3 \xrightarrow{\quad R_3 \quad} P_2$$

would create a cycle.

4.10.2. Distributed implementation

We assume that the various resources R_i are located at different sites, and partition the representation of the state of the system by locating, on each site s, the variables I_i which describe the resources which that site controls and the A_k which contain these resources. We introduce the concept of the **local view** $\mathcal{B}_s$, meaning the view which site s has of the complete graph of $\mathcal{B}$ and which consists of those arcs which site s can construct, using the information it has.

Suppose the three resources are located on three different sites S_1, S_2 and S_3 and that at S_3, for example, it is known that R_3 is included in the claim of P_2 and of P_3, and that it has not yet been allocated to either. The allocation of R_3 to P_3 would create the arc:

$$P_3 \xrightarrow{\quad R_3 \quad} P_2$$

It is therefore clear that conditions expressed in the form:

$condition_s$ (GET_i): $I_i = 0$ **and** *'this allocation will not produce a*
cycle in the graph of $\mathcal{B}_s$'

do not imply the abstract condition (1).

In view of this lack of information available at a single site, we are led to seek stronger local conditions. We now define relation $\mathcal{G}$ by:

$$P_{k1} \; \mathcal{G} \; P_{k2} \; \textit{iff} \; P_{k1} \; \mathcal{B} \; P_{k2} \; \textit{or} \; k1 < k2$$

and denote by $\mathcal{G}_s$ the local view of $\mathcal{G}$ at site s. It can be shown that the following holds:

the absence of a cycle in the graph of $\mathcal{G}_s$, for all s,
implies the absence of a cycle in the graph of $\mathcal{B}$ (2)

To prove this, it is sufficient to show that if there is a cycle in the graph of $\mathcal{B}$ then there must be a cycle in the graph of at least one $\mathcal{G}_s$. Instead of giving a formal proof, as in [Lomet 78], we shall use the present example as an illustration. At S_3 we have, because of the static ordering of the process

$$P_2 \xrightarrow{\;\;<\;\;} P_3$$

Allocating R_3 to P_3, which would give a cycle in the graph of $\mathcal{B}$, would also give a cycle in a graph of $\mathcal{G}_s$ because at S_3 it is known that R_3 is included in the claim A_2 of P_2. At S_2, however, the allocation of R_2 to P_2 would not be accepted, because:

$$P_1 \xrightarrow{\;\;<\;\;} P_2$$

and it is known at S_2 that R_2 is included in the claim of P_1. Allocating R_2 to P_1 would therefore result in the cycle:

in the local view $\mathcal{G}_2$. The graph of $\mathcal{B}$ would not, however, contain a cycle. Proposition (2) is, therefore, an implication rather than an equivalence.

Proposition (2) allows us to adopt the following local conditions for synchronization:

$condition_s$ (GET_i): $I_i = 0$ **and** *'this allocation will not produce a*
cycle in the graph of $\mathcal{G}_s$'

4.10.3. Extensions of the treatment

This rather academic example can be developed into a more realistic situation in which the processes are created dynamically. All we need to do is:

(1) Assign a unique number to each process as it is created.

(2) Broadcast the claims and require acknowledgement; a process can start when it has received the last acknowledgement.

(3) Ensure that no inconsistency in the representation of the state of the system can result from the simultaneous introduction of several processes, as might be caused by interleaving broadcasts of claims.

Clearly, the logical times at which the processes are created can be used as the numbers required in (1); and (3) will hold if all the sites acknowledge the claims in the same order.

4.11. Illustration 5: organizing access to a distributed file

This example provides another illustration of the method of partition of the variables, here in connection with accessing a distributed file [Rosenkrantz 78].

4.11.1. Analysis of the problem

The solution of the 'reader/writer' synchronization problem aims at producing a method of working which is equivalent to one in which the processes operate in serial order, where each process has the impression that it is the only user of the file. We say that the organization of the processes is one which takes account of the need for consistency among the items of information.

We study here an algorithm which pursues these aims within the following general framework:

(H1) The architecture consists of a large number N of interconnected sites, with no common memory.

(H2) A file F is a collection of partitions F_1, F_2, ... F_N, with partition F_i located on site S_i.

(H3) The processes P_k perform simple reading and writing operations on partitions F_i, determined dynamically. A process P_k is said to be a writer if at least one of its accesses is a writing operation.

(H4) Because of the large size of N, the sets of partitions accessed by any two processes will usually be disjoint.

Each process P_k can be started on any site and, in the course of its operation, creates processes at other sites for the purpose of accessing the partitions: speaking loosely, we shall include all these under the name of the original process P_k.

We shall study the case of write operations only (generalization to include reading involves detailed analysis but introduces no new problems). The synchronization points are $STARTWRITE_i$ (first access to F_i) and $ENDWRITE_i$ (last access to F_i). The following rules are imposed:

(a) A process has exclusive access to F_i between $STARTWRITE_i$ and $ENDWRITE_i$: this is to ensure consistency in F_i.

(b) Once a process has released a partition it cannot seize another; otherwise, it could use the information which it now knows that partition to contain (and which could be modified by another process) to modify the newly acquired partition. Consequently, the consistency of the partitions could not be guaranteed. The following constraint is therefore imposed:

> All the $ENDWRITE_i$ operations are performed immediately before the termination of P.

It follows that for any process P there is an instant at which it, and it alone, has possession of all the partitions which it needs; and, therefore, that the working of the system as a whole is equivalent to the serial execution of the set of constituent processes.

For the same reasons as apply to Illustration 4 (section 4.10), there is a risk of deadlock here, as shown in Fig. 10.

Taking (H4) into account, it seems too costly, in the absence of more information on the detailed behaviour of the processes than is given in (H3), to ensure complete prevention of deadlock. Instead, a method for alleviating the situation, when it arises, can be provided, involving 'killing' one or more processes. To make it possible to kill and then to revive a process, the required accesses are made to copies of the partitions, these being destroyed if the process suffers premature death, but if it survives to the first EN-$DWRITE_i$ they replace the originals and the process is declared indestructible — meaning that it is now certain that this process will run to its end.

The conditions for crossing the points $STARTWRITE_i$ are of type WRI-TER applied to partition F_i. However, the delaying of processes waiting to cross these points is accompanied by the execution of a procedure for detection and resolution of **actual conflicts**, meaning the creation of deadlocking loops, as in Fig. 10.

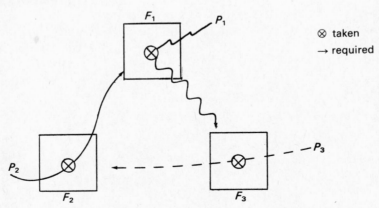

Fig. 10. *Example of deadlock.*

4.11.2. Distributed implementation

Since the conditions for allowing a process to make an access it has requested involve only the state of partition F_i, it is only in connection with the procedure for detection and resolution of conflicts that problems of distribution arise. At any one site there is a lack of information about the states of the partitions located at other sites and therefore more stringent criteria must be applied; this can be done by means of a procedure for detection and resolution of **potential** conflicts, as follows.

DETECTION

We say there is a potential conflict between processes P_{k1} and P_{k2} at site i if and only if

> P_{k2} is using partition F_i
> *and* P_{k1} is requesting this partition

Note: This definition has to be modified if there are *READ* operations, because simultaneous requests by two processes to read the same partition do not present a potential conflict.

RESOLUTION

Note first that in the case of an actual conflict, all the nodes in a deadlocking loop will have detected a potential conflict; all that is necessary, therefore, is for decisions to be taken which are consistent and which bring about the breaking of the loop. There are two possible strategies, both requiring each process to carry a logical time: here, we use the notation P_t to denote the process having logical time t. The strategies are:

(1) 'WAIT-DIE':   the last process to arrive (P_{k1}) at the synchronization point is killed if it is the youngest, otherwise it is made to wait. Thus, if the processes are P_{t1} and P_{t2}, with $t_1 > t_2$, then P_{t1} is killed.

(2) 'WOUND-WAIT':   the last to arrive is halted if it is the youngest; if not, the other is killed.

Each of these policies favours the older process if there is an actual deadlock. At least one of the processes in the loop will die, with the result that the deadlock is removed. Decisions on the killing of processes can, however, be taken without there being an actual deadlock, so preventive action can be taken.

As an illustration of the application of these strategies, consider the following pair of processes:

P_1	P_2
$a\colon F_1 := 1$	$c\colon F_4 := 2$
$b\colon F_2 := 1$	$c\colon F_3 := 2$
$f\colon F_3 := 1$	$c\colon F_2 := 2$

The only allowable results for the final state of F are those equivalent to executing $(P_1; P_2)$ sequentially in this order, giving:

$$(F_1 = 1, F_2 = 2, F_3 = 2, F_4 = 2)$$

or, in the order $(P_2; P_1)$, giving:

$$(F_1 = 1, F_2 = 1, F_3 = 1, F_4 = 2)$$

Suppose the executions take place in the order a, b, c, d: there is no conflict up to this point. When e is reached, P_2 comes into conflict with P_1 for access to F_2. If 'WAIT-DIE' is adopted, the following actions take place:

— P_2 is the last to arrive but, being older, it waits.

— P_1 continues to the point f, where it comes into conflict with P_2 for F_3.

— P_1 is now the last arriving and, being the younger of the conflicting pair, is therefore killed.

— P_2 continues to its end.

If 'WOUND-WAIT' were adopted, the detection of the conflict for F_2 would result in the immediate death of P_1.

Bibliography

[ASRM 83] Reference Manual for the Ada Programming Language; ANSI/ MIL-STD-1815A, Honeywell and Alsys, Paris, Jan. 1983.

[Brinch Hansen 72] P. BRINCH HANSEN: *A comparison of two synchronizing concepts*; Acta Informatica, **1**, 190-199, 1972.

[Brinch Hansen 73] P. BRINCH HANSEN: Operating System Principles; 1973, Prentice-Hall, Englewood Cliffs, New Jersey.

[Campbell 74] R.H. CAMPBELL: *The specification of process synchronization by path expressions*; IRIA Colloquium on Operating Systems, pp. 93-106, 1974.

[Carvalho 81] O.S.F. CARVALHO and G. ROUCAIROL: *Une amélioration de l'algorithme d'exclusion mutuelle de Ricart et Agrawala*; Report 81.58, L.I.T.P., Paris, Nov. 1981.

[Carvalho 82] O.S.F. CARVALHO and G. ROUCAIROL: *On the distribution of an assertion*; ACM-SIGACT-SIGCOPS Symposium on Principles of Distributed Computing, Ottawa, Aug. 1982.

[Cornafion 81] CORNAFION (collective name): *Systèmes informatiques répartis: concepts et techniques,* 1981, Dunod, France.

[Courtois 71] P.J. COURTOIS, F. HEYMANS and D.L. PARNAS: *Concurrent control with readers and writers*, CACM, **14** (10), Oct. 1971.

[Dijkstra 68] E.W. DIJKSTRA: *Cooperating sequential processes;* In: Programming Languages, F. Genuys (Ed.), 1968, Academic Press, New York.

[Dijkstra 71] E.W. DIJKSTRA: *Hierarchical ordering of sequential processes*; Acta Informatica, **1**, 115-138, 1971.

[Dijkstra 74] E.W. DIJKSTRA: *Self-stabilizing systems in spite of distributed control*; Comm. ACM, **17** (11), Nov. 1974.

[Flon 76] L. FLON and A.N. HABERMANN: *Towards the construction of verifiable software systems*; Proc. of Conf. on Data, Sigplan Notices, **2**, 141-148, March 1976.

[Habermann 75] A.N. HABERMANN: *Path expressions*; Research Report, Carnegie-Mellon University, 1975.

[Herman 79] D. HERMAN and J.P. VERJUS: *An algorithm for maintaining the consistency of multiple copies*; 1st Int. Conf. on Distributed Computing Systems, Huntsville, Oct. 1979.

[Herman 81] D. HERMAN: *Contrôle réparti des synchronisations entre processus*; 2nd International Conf. on Distributed Systems, Versailles, April 1981.

[Hewitt 77] C. HEWITT and H. BAKER: *Laws for communicating parallel processes*; Proc. of IFIP Congress, pp. 987-992, 1977, North-Holland, Amsterdam.

[Hewitt 79] C. HEWITT and R.R. ATKINSON: *Specification and proof techniques for serializers*; IEEE Transactions on Soft. Eng., **SE5** (1), 10-23, Jan. 1979.

[Hoare 72] C.A.R. HOARE: *Towards a theory of parallel programming*; In: Operating Systems Techniques, Hoare and Perrot (Eds), 1972, Academic Press, London.

[Hoare 74] C.A.R. HOARE: *Monitors: an operating system structuring concept*; Comm. ACM, **17** (11), 549-557, Oct. 1974.

[Howard 76] J.H. HOWARD: *Proving monitors*; Comm. ACM, **19** (5), 273-279, May 1976.

[Ichbiah 79] J. ICHBIAH et al.: *Rationale for the design of the ADA programming language*; SIGPLAN Notices, **14** (6), June 1979.

[Kaneko 79] A. KANEKO, Y. NISHIHARA, K. TSURVOKA and M. HATTORI: *Logical clock synchronization method for duplicated database control*; 1st Int. Conf. on Distributed Computing Systems, Huntsville, Oct. 1979.

[Kessel 77] J.L.W. KESSEL: *An alternative to event queues for synchronization in monitors*; Comm. ACM, **20** (7), 500-503, July 1977.

[Lamport 78] L. LAMPORT: *Time, clocks and the ordering of events in a distributed system*; Comm. ACM, **21** (7), July 1978.

[Lamport 79] L. LAMPORT: *A new approach to proving the correctness of multiprocess programs*; Comm. ACM TOPLAS, **1** (1), July 1979.

[La Palme 80] G. LA PALME: *Une implantation efficace de l'ordonnancement conditionnel*; PhD thesis, Publication no. 370, Département d'Informatique et de Recherche Opérationnelle, Montreal University, April 1980.

[Latteux 80] M. LATTEUX: *Synchronisation de processus*; RAIRO, **14** (2), 1980.

[Lauer 75] P.E. LAUER and R.H. CAMPBELL: *Formal semantics of a class of high-level primitives for coordinating concurrent processes*; Acta Informatica, **5**, 297-332, 1975.

[Le Guernic 79] P. LE GUERNIC and M. RAYNAL: *L'expression du contrôle des accès concurrents aux objets*; Bulletin AFCET Groplan, **8**, 147-197, 1979.

[Le Lann 77] G. LE LANN: *Distributed systems: towards a formal approach*; IFIP, 1977.

[Le Lann 78] G. LE LANN: *Algorithms for distributed data-sharing systems which use tickets*; 3rd Berkeley Workshop on Distributed Data Management and Computer Networks, Aug. 1978.

[Le Verrand 85] D. LE VERRAND (collective name): Evaluating Ada; 1985, North Oxford Academic, Oxford.

[Lomet 78] D. LOMET: *Coping with deadlock in distributed systems*; Report RC 7460, T.J. Watson Research Center, Sept. 1978.

[Mossière 77] J. MOSSIERE, M. TCHUENTE and J.P. VERJUS: *Sur l'exclusion mutuelle dans les réseaux informatiques*; IRISA, Internal report no. 75, 1977.

[Owicki 76] S. OWICKI and D. GRIES: *Verifying properties of parallel programs: an axiomatic approach*; Comm. ACM, **19** (5), 279-285, May 1976.

[Price 74] W.L. PRICE: *Simulation studies of an isarithmically controlled store and forward data communication network*; IFIP, pp. 151-154, 1974.

[Pulou 78] J. PULOU: *Un outil pour la spécification de la synchronisation dans les langages de haut niveau*; RAIRO, **12** (4), 291-306, 1978.

[Reed 79] R.P. REED and R.K. KANODIA: *Synchronization with event counts and sequencers*; Comm. ACM, **22** (2), Feb. 1979.

[Ricart 81] G. RICART and A. AGRAWALA: *An optimal algorithm for mutual exclusion*; Computer Network CACM, **24** (1), Jan. 1981.

[Robert 77] P. ROBERT and J.P. VERJUS: *Towards autonomous description of synchronization modules*; Proc. IFIP Congress, pp. 981-986, 1977, North-Holland, Amsterdam.

[Rosenkrantz 78] D. ROSENKRANTZ, R. STEARNS and P. LEWIS: *System level concurrency control for distributed database systems*; ACM Transactions on Database Systems, **3** (2), June 1978.

[Roucairol 78] G.P. ROUCAIROL: *Mots de synchronisation*; RAIRO, **12** (4), 277-290, 1978.

[Schmid 76] H.A. SCHMID: *On the efficient implementation of conditional critical regions and the construction of monitors*; Acta Informatica, **6**, 1976.

[Sintzoff 75] M. SINTZOFF and A. VAN LAMSWEERDE: *Constructing correct and efficient concurrent programs*; Conf. on Reliable Software, Los Angeles, pp. 319-326, 1975.

[Verjus 78] J.P. VERJUS: *Expression du contrôle à l'aide d'invariants*; Bulletin AFCET Groplan, **4**, 7-24, 1978.

[West 77] C.H. WEST: *A general technique for communication protocol validation*; IBM Journal of Research and Development, 1977.

Bibliographic note

Three general works contain a very full bibliography of the various issues raised by this book. In [Bochman 83] the area covered has been broken down into separate chapters, and the very full lists of articles given often contain valuable comments; the other two works [Paker 83; Lamport 81] are collections of articles giving fairly good coverage of the distributed system field, and each article contains its own list of references. These works therefore list the major contributions to this field of study up to 1982.

Since then, various authors have published works in this field. We have made no attempt either to survey them all or even to classify them. It is, however, worth pointing out a number of articles which seem particularly relevant to the field covered by our own book.

(a) Languages for the expression and implementation of parallelism: [Liskov 83]

(b) Atomic actions in distributed systems: [Reed 83]

(c) Description of a distributed system: [Walker 83]

(d) Taking temporal constraints into account in the specification of synchronized systems: [Caspi 82]

Finally, four international conferences on distributed systems have taken place since 1979 (the proceedings are published by the IEEE). They tend to be chiefly concerned with the methodological and practical issues involved in the design and implementation of distributed systems. At a more theoretical level (concerned with semantics and models of parallelism, or the proof of parallel programs), there is an annual international conference on parallel processing, whose proceedings are also published by the IEEE.

[Bochman 83] G.V. Bochman: Concepts for Distributed Systems Design; 1983, Springer-Verlag.

[Caspi 82] P. Caspi and N. Halbwachs: *Algebra of events: a model for parallel and real time systems*; International Conference on Parallel Processing, Bellaire, Aug. 1982.

[Lampson 81] B.W. Lampson et al.: *Distributed systems — architecture and implementation; an advanced course*; Vol. 105, 1981, Springer-Verlag.

[Liskov 83] B. Liskov and M. Herlihy: *Issues in process and communication structure for distributed programs*; 3rd Symposium on Reliability in Distributed Software and Database Systems, Clearwater Beach, Florida, 17-19 October, 1983.

[Paker 83] Y. Paker and J.P. Verjus (Eds): Distributed Computing Systems. Synchronization, Control and Communication; Nov. 1983, Academic Press, London.

[Reed 83] D.P. REED: *Implementing atomic actions on decentralized data*; ACM Transactions on Computer Systems, **1** (1), Feb. 1983.

[Walker 83] B. WALKER, G. POPEK, R. ENGLISH, C. KLINE and G. THIEL: *The locus distributed operating systems*; Proceedings of the 9th ACM Symposium on Operating Systems Principles, Bretton Woods, New Hampshire, 10-13 Oct. 1983.

Index

abstract conditions
  strengthening 73–74
abstract expression 10, 12, 15–33, 46
  calculations with 13–15
  definition 18
  for centralized system 55–61
  languages for 20–29, 78–79
abstract synchronization condition 81
accept statement 52
access critical resource 29
active wait 37, 43
Ada 6, 7, 51–53, 66
atomic access operation 35, 37, 41–42
automatic optimization 47–48
automaton 20, 21, 32
  finite state 21, 26, 27, 29

binary relations between pairs of events 17
blocked processes 39–40
blocking calls 53
Boolean expressions 50–51
buffer space 1
buffers 36, 37, 66, 70

car park problem 90
centralized control 83, 91
centralized implementation 5–8, 34–61
centralized system, abstract expression for 55–61
coherence 3, 34, 35, 38, 86
common-memory systems 35
commutative operations 94
competition between processes 90
competitive interactions 1
compiler 53, 55
concurrent events 18
condition operation 50
condition variables 49
conditional wait 52, 53
conditions 34
consistency 68
  among copies of the same information 95–96
constraints imposed by synchronization 17
consumer 36
control languages 21
control message 69
control modules 25–26, 33, 36, 56, 78
control processes 63
control sequences, mutually exclusive 42–43
control statements 39–40
controller 22, 25, 56
  explicit 6
  implicit 7
  parallel operation of 11–12
  role of 5, 6, 8, 19
  use of term 1
cooperating processes 39, 44, 46
cooperative interactions 1
counters 25, 46, 64
  decomposition of monotonically-increasing 78–86
  monotonically-increasing 92
critical regions 44, 53, 54, 57
  conditional 45

unconditional 45
critical resource 29
critical section, definition 42
cyclic processes 22

deadlock
  definition 13–14
  example of 101
  impossibility of 13–14
  occurrence of 28, 29, 43, 84
  prevention of 46, 97–100
delays 19
disabling relation 47–48
distributed architecture 62, 64
distributed control 10–12, 63, 91
  implementation of 72
distributed file, accessing 100–3
distributed implementation 34, 62–103
  management of approximate representations 81–86
distributed systems 19
  order of events in 70
  scheduling in 70–72
  synchronization constraints 86

empty 49
enabling relation 47–48
end consumer 37
end producer 36, 37
entry point 48, 52
equitability 68, 70
equity 21, 29, 30
events 2
  date of 17
  minimizing number of 18
  observable 9
  observation of 63
  ordering 68–70
  simultaneous 18
extended control modules 29, 33

GET 1

Hoare's problem 31, 32, 60

implementation techniques 19–20, 38–41
independence 19
infinite wait 14–15, 93
information exchange 1
integer variables 56
interpreters 53, 54
invariant 5, 23, 64
iteration 26

journals 32

Kessel's condition 50–51

Lamport's algorithm 71
local conditions 73, 74
local limits
  decreasing 84
  increasing 83
local view concept 98
logical clocks 71–72